THIRD RAIL

THE POETRY OF ROCK AND ROLL

EDITED BY JONATHAN WELLS

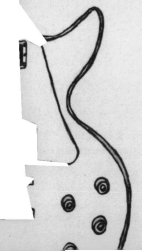

  BOOKS

POCKET BOOKS MTV BOOKS

New York London Toronto Sydney

DEDICATION

THANKS TO THE PEOPLE who contributed in one way or another: Chris Merrill, Marie Ponsot, Paul Muldoon, David St. John, Poets House, Bill Flanagan, Mike Corbett, Judy McGrath, Reuben Napkine, Kurt Brown, Matthew Zapruder, Michael Zilkha, Paul McGuinness, Karen Glenn, Susan Hunter, Jacob Hoye, Lollion Chong, and Jennifer Heddle.

To Jane for her love and patience and Alexander, Juliet, Delilah, and Gabriel for their good questions.

CONTENTS

FOREWORD BY BONO   XI

INTRODUCTION BY JONATHAN WELLS   XIII

Busking, **KEVIN YOUNG**   1

Guns N' Roses, **CAMPBELL MCGRATH**   3

An Elegy for Bob Marley, **WILLIAM MATTHEWS**   9

The Musician Talks About Process, **RITA DOVE**   11

Interlude: Still Still, **ROBIN BEHN**   13

Decrescendo, **LARRY LEVIS**   17

Cheers, **BILLY COLLINS**   20

Truncated Elegy, **MARK BIBBINS**   23

Kissing and Telling, **PAUL MULDOON**   24

Listening to Jefferson Airplane, **THOM GUNN**   25

The Hallelujah Jam, **VICTORIA REDEL**   26

The Reef, **DAVID ST. JOHN**   28

The Wailers in Estadio Nacional, **IDRA NOVEY**   30

At the Fillmore, **PHILIP LEVINE**   32

Days of 1968, **EDWARD HIRSCH**   35

Dream Job, **MATTHEW ZAPRUDER**   36

Alas, They Sighed, You Were Not Like Us, **SARAH MANGUSO**   39

If Poetry Were Not Morality, **TESS GALLAGHER**   40

Portrait of a Lady, **ALAN JENKINS**   44

A Repertoire, **MICHAEL DONAGHY**   45

A Genesis Text for Larry Levis, Who Died Alone, **NORMAN DUBIE**   47

Sun-Saddled, Coke-Copping, Bad-Boozing Blues,

   CHARLES WRIGHT   50

Golden Oldie, **RITA DOVE**   52

Endless Sleep, **KURT BROWN**   53

Household Gods, **JIM ELLEDGE**   57

Phantom, **STEPHEN DUNN**   59

Love Potion No. 9, **ROBERT LONG**   61

Parkersburg, **MARK HALLIDAY**   63

Elvis's Twin Sister, **CAROL ANN DUFFY**   65

Elvis Presley, **THOM GUNN**   67

The Wine Talks, **JAMES TATE**   68

The Sun Sessions, **LAVINIA GREENLAW**   70

Shore Leave, **LYNDA HULL**   71

Cher, **DORIANNE LAUX**   74

Chiffon, **LYNDA HULL**   76

Annus Mirabilis, **PHILIP LARKIN**   80

The Assassination of John Lennon as Depicted by the Madame

   Tussaud Wax Museum, Niagara Falls, Ontario, 1987,

   DAVID WOJAHN   82

Yeah Yeah Yeah, **RODDY LUMSDEN**   84

From Me to You, **ROBYN FIALKOW**   85

Bed Music, **CHARLES SIMIC**   87

Rock Music, **DEREK MAHON**   88

North(west)ern, **PATIENCE AGBABI**   90

Some Crazy Dancing, **VICTORIA REDEL**   91

Disco Elegy, **DANIEL TOBIN**   93

I Like the Music That Shakes, **JONATHAN WELLS**   95

Delivering Eggs to the Girls' Dorm, **B. H. FAIRCHILD**   97

An Englishman Abroad, **AUGUST KLEINZAHLER**   99

Hanoi Hannah, **YUSEF KOMUNYAKAA**   103

Ooly Poop a Cow, **DAVID HUDDLE**   105

Sleep, After Ray Charles Show and Hurricane Report,

    HEATHER MCHUGH   107

Sleeve Notes, **PAUL MULDOON**   108

The Burning of the Midnight Lamp, **EDWARD HIRSCH**   120

Electric Church, **WILLIAM OLSEN**   124

All Along the Watchtower, **TONY HOAGLAND**   128

Between Takes, **PAUL MULDOON**   131

Watching Young Couples with an Old Girlfriend on Sunday Morning,

    AUGUST KLEINZAHLER   132

Montage: MTV, **YUSEF KOMUNYAKAA**   133

The Victim, **THOM GUNN**   134

Punk Rock You're My Big Crybaby, **ALLEN GINSBERG**   136

Rock Music, **LES MURRAY**   137

"What's So Funny 'Bout Peace, Love and Understanding,"

    ROBERT LONG   138

Manhattan Diptych, **DAVID ST. JOHN**   140

Lucifer in Starlight, **DAVID ST. JOHN**   142

C Train Home: Lou Reed After the Wake of Delmore Schwartz, July 1966,

    DAVID WOJAHN   145

7-Minute Song, **MARK BIBBINS**   146

The Prophet's Song, **DANIEL NESTER**   147

The Prophecy, **ROBERT WRIGLEY**   148

Bohemian Rhapsody, **DANIEL NESTER**   151

Vince Neil Meets Josh in a Chinese Restaurant in Malibu
    (After Exra Pound),
    JOSH BELL   152

Variation on a Theme by Whitesnake, **DAN HOY**   155

The Secret History of Rock & Roll,
    CHARLES HARPER WEBB   156

Mostly Mick Jagger, **CATIE ROSEMURGY**   159

Necromancy: The Last Days of Brian Jones, 1968,
    DAVID WOJAHN   162

Gimme Shelter, **BILL KNOTT**   163

The Penalty for Bigamy Is Two Wives, **WILLIAM MATTHEWS**   165

You Can't Rhumboogie in a Ball and Chain, **ALICE FULTON**   167

Pearl, **DORIANNE LAUX**   169

Berkeley 1971, **KAREN GLENN**   171

Blue Lonely Dreams, **MARC COHEN**   173

Comebacks, **CHARLES HARPER WEBB**   179

Birthday, **FRANZ WRIGHT**   181

POET BIOGRAPHIES   183

CREDITS   197

FOREWORD
BY BONO

THE POETS WHO FILL the pews here have come to testify, to bear witness to the mysterious power of Rock and Roll. Their lives have at some point been upended by guitar, bass, and drum. They are evangelists and hopeless addicts. . . . drunks in Leonard Cohen's midnight choir, gate-crashers at Midnight Mass on Christmas Eve, whispering in high spirits. These men and women are rowdy but around the corner from tears.

Rock and Roll is truly a broad church, but each lights a candle to their vision of what it is. Some write of their first love, some are still in love with their first love (I am one of those). It's an unexplainable feeling like, Faith. . . It occupies a place that the less we visit, the less alive we feel. It is not about youth but the evidence of life.

All the writers in Jonathan Wells's *Third Rail* march to the tattoo best explained by Bob Dylan, ". . . he not busy being born is busy dying." They know that demise starts with your record collection.

INTRODUCTION
BY JONATHAN WELLS

SAY YOU ARE WAITING at a traffic light on a city street at ten o'clock on a humid summer night. The air-conditioning in your car doesn't work so the windows are rolled down. Another car pulls up next to you and the radio is playing Jimi Hendrix's version of "All Along the Watchtower." Loud. You listen to part of a verse then the light turns green and the car takes off in a blur. You are left behind mouthing some of the lyrics, "There must be some kind of way out of here / Said the joker to the thief . . ."

Or your telephone company puts you on hold as you are waiting to pay the bill. A soundtrack comes on that has borrowed John Lennon's "Imagine" without lyrics. You think to yourself how schmaltzy it sounds and supply the words yourself.

A variety of everyday situations offers music you have heard before, with or without lyrics, slightly rearranged to sell something, to flesh out a film or television character, to tell you your phone is ringing, or to hold your patience. The music and lyrics float into your mind and just as easily drift off. This is not deep listening and yet it is ubiquitous, subliminal, and impossible to ignore.

In many of these poems music and lyrics do the same. They enter suddenly, gracefully, and then vanish just as quickly. In Thom Gunn's poem "Listening to Jefferson Airplane" the music arrives on the wind and departs the same way. In Stephen Dunn's poem "Phantom" Bob Dylan races out of the radio and then fades away. This does not mean the song or singer is peripheral to the poem. Its appearance is as important as any other of its features.

In some poems, the song is an instrument that delivers a memory back from a forgotten time of a person, place, or event. Although the poem is carefully staged these are not *considered* moments but are just as unavoidable as the ones that come from the car next door or being put on "a brief hold." But they offer a more full-bodied experience. In Rita Dove's poem "The Musician Talks About Process" the narrator remembers his grandfather playing spoons and how he played them and where and then describes how he plays them himself, which leads to his surprising conclusion. The poem follows a longer trail into the woods.

Other poems are meditations on a song or a singer, descriptive or analytical. The subject is confronted and taken apart before being reassembled, as in Alice Fulton's poem for Janis Joplin "You Can't Rhumboogie in a Ball and Chain." Fulton's choices of language don't just describe the voice and the singer, but evoke it and place it in Fulton's context. In Campbell McGrath's apocalyptic poem "Guns N' Roses" only three minutes of a song are enough to make him remember the details of a specific time, with its distinctions, distortions, and oddities.

Many of the poems ask or answer the question, What is music? Where does it come from? For William Matthews, "music calls us together." In "Interlude: Still Still" by Robin Behn a boy looks for it inside a guitar sound hole where he had dropped a quarter as if it had been a jukebox. Outside Larry Levis's window, "the music ends, the needle on the phonograph / Scrapes like someone raking leaves, briefly, across / A sidewalk, & no one alone is, particularly, special. / That is what musicians are for, to remind us of this." And finally Franz Wright affirms what is beyond discussion, "Everyone agrees. / The dead singers have the best voices."

These poems display the range of music and an attention to it from acute listening to random moments as music appears and disappears around us. The lines of some of these poems may stay with you for an hour or a day. Hopefully, some of them will remain as long as the lyrics of songs that return without being summoned.

BUSKING

The day folds up like money
if you're lucky. Mostly

sun a cold coin
drumming into the blue

of a guitar case. Close
up & head home.

Half-hundred times I wanted
to hock these six strings

or hack, if I could, my axe
into firewood. That blaze

never lasts.
I've begged myself hoarse

sung streetcorner
& subway over a train's blast

through stale air & trash.
You've seen me, brushed past—

my strings screech
& light up like a third rail—

mornings, I am fed by flies,
strangers, sunrise.

KEVIN YOUNG

GUNS N' ROSES

I.M. TIM DWIGHT, 1958-1994

Not a mea culpa, not an apology, but an admission:
there are three minutes in the middle of "Sweet Child o' Mine"
that still, for all the chopped cotton of the passing years,
for all the muddled victories and defeats of a lifetime,
for all the grief and madness and idiocy of our days,
slay me, just slay me. They sound like how it felt to be alive
at that instant, how it was to walk the streets of Manhattan
in that era of caviar and kill-hungry feedback,
the Big Apple so candy-coated with moral slush and easy money
even the corporate heavyweights could fashion no defense
against decay, all the homeless encamped over cold coffee
at Dunkin' Donuts on upper Broadway, even McDonald's
become a refugee camp for victims of the unacknowledged war
fought beneath the giddy banners of corporatization
as the decade spun down its drain of self-delusion. *Where
do we go, where do we go, where do we go
now?* What a glorious passage, a shimmering bridge
embodying everything rock and roll aspires to be,
heroic and violent and joyous and juvenile
and throbbing with self-importance and percolating

with melodrama and thrilled and scared by
its own anthemic power, by the kid-on-a-scooter freedom
and the hill a lot steeper than it seemed at first glance,
what the hell, rust never sleeps, live and let die, etc., etc.
And whenever I hear that song, become, now,
a classic of the genre, even as it suffuses me with nostalgia
for those days of malt liquor and bbq chips,
it gives me cause to think of Axl Rose in his purgatory
self-assembled from paranoia and Malibu chaparral,
wrestling exotic demons, kickboxing with Jesus,
binding and gagging his women with duct tape in the closet,
much the way the heavy metal mentality of the times
seized and militarized his music, sonic warriors
blasting "Paradise City" at the Panamanian dictator,
"Welcome to the Jungle" for the Waco cultists,
Slash and Axl circling the globe, leveling ancient civilizations
with power chords and teenage emotions,
from the Halls of Mentholyptus to the Shores of MTV.
And if Axl appears almost Nixonian in his anguish,
at least he is not Kurt Cobain, forsaken and baby-faced
as J. Michael Pollard in the episode of *Lost in Space*
where Penny goes through the mirror to a realm
of demoniacal toys and that metaphysical bear-monster,

cousin to the troglodytes that chased Raquel Welch
up the cavern tree in *One Million Years B.C.*,
death in its many B-movie guises, so much gaudier
than the killers that walked the streets among us,
the needle and the dollar, the gun and the rose,
and the last time we saw Tim, at Bruce's place
in the Hollywood hills, he recalled the first time
we'd all hung out together in New York, Halloween, 1985,
provincial immigrants tossing back bourbon and tequila,
Tim holding a bundle of Ecstasy for some dealer—
a drug I'd never even heard of—which instead of trying to market
he handed around with cavalier generosity,
packets of powder doused in the tall cans of Colt 45
we drank as we walked the streets of the Village
amidst the disintegrating drifts and dregs of the parade,
and finally a midnight show at the Ritz, some L.A. bands
the girls adored done up in black-light fluorescents,
dancing and stage-diving, jubilant and hallucinatory,
getting home somehow on a subway serviced
by orange-vested trolls before waking to cold sweat
and hangover candy and a day of recuperation and the desire
to do it all again. Because there was plenty of time,
we knew, or thought we knew, or were simply too stupid

not to know we didn't know at all, time to waste or kill
before the crashes and commitments that would doom or save
or cast us back into the tide pools of the westering continent.
Tim was still laughing, hauntingly frail, but what I thought
looking out across the canyon was how badly
Los Angeles had aged, wanton and care-worn,
like a faded child star sickled with cosmetic surgery scars
still dreaming of a comeback, still scheming and groveling,
as if to prove that nothing really dies in America
but is merely removed from the shelves for repackaging,
coming back crisper and crunchier, cholesterol-free,
as even Axl Rose is coming back with Tommy Stinson on bass
and a sideman wearing a KFC bucket like a Spartan helmet,
and I wish that I could lay the blame for Axl's fucked-up life
on the feral orphanhood of the Pax Atomica,
the alienation of lives begun with no expectation of completion,
it would be simpler that way, for all of us,
but the world did not end in a vortex of toxic fire,
the flying fortresses have returned from the stratosphere
and the missiles endure their nightmares mutely in dark silos
and we have no excuse but the arrogance of power for our narcissism
and no solace but the merciless amplitude of our din.
And that was it, the moment had passed,

another gem or tear for the cut-glass diadem of passing years.

Someone cranked the music up, someone made a toast

to the pool lights and glitter. And then the Pixies

begin some riff-rife, fully surfable rifle-shot of a theme song

announcing the ironic revival of our childhood

swaggering like Tony the Tiger atop a station wagon

at an Esso station in 1964, Tony the Tiger

back from the dead, eldritch and transcendent—

rise, the immortals!—

rise to grasp the silver handles

of the casket in procession before us, Ultraman

and Astroboy and Mr. Clean and the Man from Glad

and Josie & the Pussycats

on the Rose Bowl float with their God

Bless America batons a-twirl

and then—

huh—

cue the horns,

take it down, break it all apart

and start from nothing to garb our nakedness

with sheets of beaten gold,

cozen us with grieving blossoms,

anoint us with honey in the dry riverbed,

and tell me,

o great devourer,

o master of thorns and ashes,

where do we go

now?

CAMPBELL MCGRATH

AN ELEGY FOR BOB MARLEY

In an elegy for a musician,
one talks a lot about music,
which is a way to think about time
instead of death or Marley,

and isn't poetry itself about time?
But death is about death and not time.
Surely the real fuel for elegy
is anger to be mortal.

No wonder Marley sang so often
of an ever-arriving future, that verb tense
invented by religion and political rage.
Soon come. Readiness is all,

and not enough. From the ruinous
dust and sodden torpor
of Trenchtown, from the fruitpeels
and imprecations, from cunning,

from truculence, from the luck
to be alive, however, cruelly,

Marley made a brave music—
a rebel music, he called it,

though music calls us together,
however briefly—and a fortune.
One is supposed to praise the dead
in elegies for leaving us their songs,

though they had no choice; nor could
the dead bury the dead if we could pay
them to. This is something else we can't
control, another loss, which is, as someone

said in hope of consolation,
only temporary, though the same phrase
could be used of our lives and bodies
and all that we hope survives them.

WILLIAM MATTHEWS

THE MUSICIAN TALKS ABOUT PROCESS

AFTER ANTHONY "SPOONS" POUGH

I learned the spoons from
my grandfather, who was blind.
Every day he'd go into the woods
'cause that was his thing.
He met all kinds of creatures,
birds and squirrels,
and while he was feeding them
he'd play the spoons,
and after they finished
they'd stay and listen.

When I go into Philly
on a Saturday night,
I don't need nothing but
my spoons and the music.
Laid out on my knees
they look so quiet,
but when I pick them up
I can play to anything:
a dripping faucet,

a tambourine,
fish shining in a creek.

A funny thing:
When my grandfather died,
every creature sang.
And when the men went out
to get him, they kept singing.
They sung for two days,
all the birds, all the animals.
That's when I left the South.

RITA DOVE

INTERLUDE: STILL STILL

Inside the hole, where it's yellow,
the boy has dropped a quarter
so that the guitar rattles

when he shakes it by the neck.
Knocks, scrapes, scars.
So this is what music is.

The wooden body is no longer
bigger than his body.
The strings, which, when

he strums them,
go on forever are forever
wound around small pegs

that creak like the ones
they wrap the ropes around,
there being an absence of

able-bodied mourners

to lower, with the softer machines
of their bodies, the coffin down.

It was a cold day.
The boy had not been born yet,
but stood among us

warm in his round place.
Then, from the distance,
the bagpiper who'd been found

in the yellow pages
extracted the horizon note
like a red needle from the sky.

And so it was not with nothing
human our friend was lowered.
This is what music is.

But how did it sound to the boy,
The bladder of cries squeezed
through the slit throat

when there had not been anything
yet to cry about?
The solace of music is

not that we recognize it.
It is that the hearing
comes from before and is wound

around after. Between,
our bad singing a stranger
dozed, then bulldozed, to.

At home, in its case, the guitar
was hunkered inside the dark
into which music goes,

and the more particular dark
from which music comes
was inside of it.

The sound hole swallowed and passed back
buckets of silence
until the inner and outer dark

had the same yellow smell.
This, while the song the boy
would pay for waited, still still.

ROBIN BEHN

DECRESCENDO

If there is only one world, it is this one.

In my neighborhood, the ruby-helmeted woodpecker's line
Is all spondees, & totally formal as it tattoos
Its instinct & solitude into a high sycamore which keeps

Revising autumn until I will look out, &
Something final will be there: a branch in winter—not
Even a self-portrait. Just a thing.

Still, it is strange to live alone, to feel something
Rise up, out of the body, against all that is,
By law, falling & turning into the pointless beauty

Of calendars. Think of the one in the office closed
For forty-three summers in a novel by Faulkner, think
Of unlocking it, of ducking your head slightly
And going in. It is all pungent, & lost. Or

It is all like the doomed singers, Cooke & Redding,
Who raised their voices against the horns'

Implacable decrescendos, & knew exactly what they

Were doing, & what they were doing was dangerous.

The man on sax & the other on piano never had to argue
Their point, for their point was time itself; & all
That one wished to say, even to close friends,
One said beside that window: The trees turn; a woman
Passing on the street below turns up her collar against
The cold; &, if the music ends, the needle on the phonograph
Scrapes like someone raking leaves, briefly, across
A sidewalk, & no one alone is, particularly, special.

That is what musicians are for, to remind us of this, unless

Those singers die, one shot in a motel room
By a woman who made a mistake; & one dead
In a plane crash, an accident.

Which left a man on sax & another on piano
With no one to back up, & hearing the news,
One sat with his horn in a basement in Palo Alto,
Letting its violence go all the way up, &

Annoying the neighbors until the police came,
And arrested him—who had, in fact, tears
In his eyes. And the other, a white studio
Musician from L.A., who went home & tried

To cleave the keyboard with his hands until
They bled, & his friends came, & called his wife,
And someone went out for bandages & more bourbon—

Hoping to fix up, a little, this world.

LARRY LEVIS

CHEERS

Already tonight I have lifted my glass to Jackie
Wilson and to Gracie Lantz, the voice
of Woody Woodpecker and creator of the taunting laugh
according to her obituary in this morning's paper.

And now the wind is whistling at the doors and windows,
straining to lift the roof off this house,
and I am alone and casting about for someone else
to toast, someone remarkable whose leaving

shrivels the skin of the world. It could be
a virgin martyr or exiled Ovid, or even Jackie
Wilson again, the man no act would follow,
not James Brown, not the Temptations, one of whom

explained it was because he left a hole in the stage.
The only toast that should follow a toast to the dead
is a toast to the long dead, so up goes my glass
to the first man ever to notice the outline

of a bear in the stars one quiet night long before

the wheel and shortly after fire. It is said
that laziness was the mother of astronomy,
and surely he must have spent hours on his back,

hands pillowing his head, while his eyes
connected the points of light with imaginary lines
until a ferocious shape stood before him in the sky.
I drink to the long wonderment of his gazing,

the Nile of amazement flowing into the night,
his hand moving up to cover his open mouth
and still the wind is driving hard through the trees,
knocking down the weak branches which I will

gather in the morning and break over my knee
for kindling; but the scene inside is composed,
a tableau of bottle, vase, open book,
a painting of a little ship framed on the wall,

far from home in a churning sea and burdened
with perilous cargo. I wander in the details
of its sail lines and streamers flying from the masts.
I see a man in the rigging, the red dot of his shirt.

No wonder visitors always remark on this picture
while I am out in the kitchen making their drinks
and getting ready to propose the first toast,
to hoist my glass to that dark, bearded man

lying dumbstruck and reeking of woodsmoke
a little distance from the mouth of his cave.
Here's to the bear he saw roaring in the heavens,
to the ram, the tilted scales, the intricate crab,

and the dippers pouring out a universe of ink.
Here's to Cassiopeia in her chair and chained Andromeda.
Here's to the wind blowing against this lighted house
and to the vast, windless spaces between the stars.

BILLY COLLINS

TRUNCATED ELEGY

Before going under   did he notice   how the sky grew
thick with the wings of birds   or taste the rust of lungs   the ache

We wait by the delta for a drunken boy to return
leaving our doors unlocked in case his longing exceeds us

To have shifted abandon   into something tangible—
a manna to prevail against cognition's undertow

Flower in his teeth   love sung to his own end   and the dark
he drifted through   like the moon burning   up a merlot sky

JEFF BUCKLEY (1966–1997)

MARK BIBBINS

KISSING AND TELLING

Or she would turn up *The Songs of Leonard Cohen*
on the rickety old gramophone.

And you knew by the way she unbound her tresses
and stepped from her William Morris dresses

you might just as well be anyone.

Goat's-milk cheeses, Navajo rugs,
her reading aloud from *A Dictionary of Drugs*—

she made wine of almost everything.

How many of those she found out on the street
and fetched back to her attic room—

to promise nothing, to take nothing for granted—

how many would hold by the axiom
she would intone as though it were her mantra?

I could name names. I could be indiscreet.

PAUL MULDOON

LISTENING TO JEFFERSON AIRPLANE

IN THE POLO GROUNDS, GOLDEN GATE PARK

The music comes and goes on the wind,
Comes and goes on the brain.

THOM GUNN

THE HALLELUJAH JAM

What decoy praise is this night,
Sunday at a West Side dive
where nothing's left of Saturday's mix
but the guy scraping air guitar to Layla's riff
and the girl yanking off
her boyfriend's Bill Clinton mask.

Glory them in the misfit light—
they're pals, our buds tonight
kind enough not to stare
at our middle-aged rocker's groove,
hip to hip, we're stunning
runaways, blocks from the bus terminal.

If weeks from now there's almost nothing
left of us but old neighborhoods
where walking down the street we'll face ourselves,
then let others go after the shifting moon
or croon for the distant stars
on their wobbled axis.

Let for us the eternity jukebox play it again—
this hallelujah jam in love
with midnight doorways, the imprint
of your face knocked up close to mine.
Praise the human pulse, praise joy, baby,
a shake-it dance floor. Praise praise.
Praise it. Truth. Come closer.

VICTORIA REDEL

THE REEF

The most graceful of misunderstandings
I could not keep close at hand
She paused a moment
At the door as she adjusted her scarf again
The winds & sprays & in the moonlight
She rowed back across the inlet to the shore

I sat alone above my pale vodka
Watching its smoky trails of peppercorns
Rising toward my lips

& while I flicked the radio dial
Trying to pick up the Cuban station or even
The static of "The Reggae Rooster" from Jamaica

I watched the waves foam above the coral & recede

Then foam breathlessly again & again
As a school of yellowtail
Rose together to the surface & then suddenly dove
Touched I knew by the long silver glove

Of the barracuda she loved to watch each afternoon
As she let the boat drift in its endlessly

Widening & broken arc

DAVID ST. JOHN

THE WAILERS IN ESTADIO NACIONAL

ONCE PINOCHET'S PROVISIONAL DETENTION CENTER

Before the concert, Ziggy Marley
says it again, *for the detained,*
tortured in this stadium—we play
for you.

       Two bare-chested boys
lift their joints and shout the name
of an uncle. Where I lie on a blanket,
everyone standing looks tall, hands
easy in their pockets—no way to tell
who was conceived under curfew
and who in exile, returned now
from East Berlin.

           Ziggy says
the first song's about democracy—
the lyrics in English, message
turned to cadence, to the grind and nick
of hips along the pocked wall, wheels
of the slow machine

              that is a country.
The oval sky above the stadium

dims, dusky—the cut purple
of Santiago smog and summer,
of plums. He starts another song,
stating only, *this is not my father's.*

IDRA NOVEY

AT THE FILLMORE

The music was going on.
The soldier paced outside
his shoes slowly filling

with rain. Morning
would walk early
over the wards of the wounded,

row after row
of small white faces
dragged back.

She dozed in the Ladies
wondering should she
return. This warmth

like the flush of juice
up the stale stem
of the flower, she'd known

before, and its aftermath—

seeing the Sisters
and the promises again.

The music was going on,
a distant pulsing only
from the wilderness of strobes.

He climbed back up
the crowded stairs cloaked
in a halo of rain, and no one

noticed or called.
Nor were those the waters
of the heart she heard

rushing in the booth
beside her. She stubbed
her cigarette and rose.

The music was going on
gathering under
the turning lights, mounting

in the emptying hall
toward the end. They stood
blinded a moment,

and then she offered herself
to his arms and opened
her arms to him, both

of them smiling as they
claimed the other
and whatever else was theirs.

PHILIP LEVINE

DAYS OF 1968

She came to me with a mind like fire
and a name written in smoky letters on the wind.

She came to me with the grief of a fallen angel,
with white arms that should have been wings

and skinny legs sadly rooted to the ground.
She came to me barefoot in a sleeveless dress,

playing air guitar and talking about the gods
who said she never should have been saddled

with a body in the first place, with a human
past and a disembodied voice flickering

like a small candle in the endless dark.
"I believe in being reincarnated," she declared—

my pure psyche, my haunted half-girl turning
back into the spirit she wanted to become.

EDWARD HIRSCH

DREAM JOB

Today abstracted
as a glass of milk
forgotten by a kid who went
into this interminable
rain to play, I was reading
up on the science of tracking
the movement of birds
through spring. It seems
just as for us says Professor
Martin Wikelski of Princeton
who each night for six weeks
with his team of researchers
captured and carefully
injected thrushes with double-
labeled water ampules,
for the birds a long
spring flight is painless
relative to the fighting
at rest areas that can really
drain the migrating out of you.
I have so many questions.

First the doubly labeled
water technique. If on
a cool day a bird at rest
a nonflying bird
staying warm consumes
the same kilojoules
as two-and-a-half
wind tunnel hours,
how many isotopes
does it take to tremble
in the researcher's hand?
What happens if overhead
in the clouds or laughing
at a joke about penguins
someone loses the birds?
Each morning the researchers
inject a small
portion of double water,
each evening
the blood reports,
to where they are going
the thrushes move closer,
the researchers follow,

soon they can go
back to Princeton
Twin Rivers or Hightstown,
say goodbye thrushes,
and it occurs
to me in my snow globe
surrounded with rain
on Water Street by the sea,
it's possible all this
capturing daily
was for some other purpose.
Put down the paper.
I'm sure I can see
each week the team
growing increasingly
tender holding
the small thrushes they
probably had to name.
Go, Jerry, soon you will be
in Canada where
Neil Young was born.

MATTHEW ZAPRUDER

ALAS, THEY SIGHED, YOU WERE NOT LIKE US

For once they had nothing to say about my death,
and I killed them.
After that I put on a Neil Young record in my poem because he used to
        write in fevers
and because there's something about beauty that's always going to be a
        problem.

They told me if I played "Cinnamon Girl"
enough times, they would love me.
They didn't have to hold me,
and they sent me money and macramé belts
spelling the words "Jesus" and "O To Know Your Dark Uplifted Heart."
I loved them
and I was listening to myself
and writing down what I heard.
They were pretty sure it was about them.

SARAH MANGUSO

IF POETRY WERE NOT MORALITY

IT IS LIKELY I WOULD NOT HAVE DEVOTED MYSELF TO POETRY IN THIS WORLD

WHICH REMAINS INSENSITIVE TO IT, IF POETRY WERE NOT A MORALITY.

—*JEAN COCTEAU,* PAST TENSE

I'm the kind of woman who
when she hears Bobby McFerrin sing without words
for the first time on the car radio has to
pull over and park with the motor
running. And Cecil Taylor, I pulled over
for him too, even though later the guy
at the record store said he was just
a "side man". Something he did with silence and
mixing classical with I'm-worried-about-this-but-I-
have-to-go-this-way-anyhow. *This* not letting me
go. What did you do, the guy asked me, when you
pulled over? Smiled, I said, sat

and smiled. If the heart could be that simple. The photo
of Gandhi's last effects taped near
my typewriter: eyeglasses, sandals, writing paper
and pen, low lap-sized writing desk and something

white in the foreground like a bedroll.
Every so often I glance at this, just paper torn
from a book, and wish I could get down to
that, a few essentials, no
more. So when I left this place it would be
humbly, as in those welfare funerals my mother
used to scorn because the county always bought

the cheapest coffins, no satin lining, and if you
wanted the dead to look comfortable
you had to supply your own
pillow. I still admire her hating to see the living
come off cheap in their homage to any life. She
was Indian enough so the kids used to
taunt me home with "Your mother's a squaw!"
Cherokee, she said. And though nobody
told me, I knew her grandfather had to be
one of those chiefs who could never

get enough horses. Who, if he had two hundred,
wanted a hundred more and a hundred more
after that. Maybe he'd get up in the night and go
out among them, or watch their grazing

from a distance under moonlight. He'd pass his mind
over them where they pushed their muzzles into
each other's flanks and necks and their horseness
gleamed back at him like soundless music until
he knew something he couldn't know
as only himself, something not to be told again
even by writing down the doing

of it. I meet him like that sometimes,
wordless and perfect, with more horses than he
can ride or trade or even know why
he has. His completeness needs to be stern, measuring
what he stands to lose. His eyes
are bronze, his heart is bronze with the mystery
of it. Yet it will change his sleep
to have gazed beyond memory, I think, without sadness or
fear onto the flowing backs of horses. I look down
and see that his feet are bare, and I
have never seen such beautiful prideless feet set
on the earth. He must know what he's doing, I think, he
must not need to forgive himself the way I do

because this bounty pours onto me
so I'm crushed by surrender, heaped and

scattered and pounded into the dust with wanting more,
wanting feet like that to drive back
the shame that wants to know why
I have to go through the world like an overwrought
magnet, like the greedy Braille of so many
about-to-be-lost memories. Why I can't just
settle down by the side of the road and turn the music
up on one of those raw uncoffined voices of
the dead—Bob Marley, Billie Holiday or the way Piaf
sang "Je Ne Regrette Rien"—so that when

the purled horse in the music asks what I want with it
we are swept aside by there being no answer except
not to be dead to each other, except for
those few moments to belong beyond deserving to
that sumptuousness of presence, so the heart
stays simple like the morality of
a robin, the weight of living so clear a mandate
it includes everything about this junkshop
of a life. And even some of our soon-to-be deadness
catches up to us
as joy, as more horses than we need.

TESS GALLAGHER

PORTRAIT OF A LADY

She's been in too deep and out too far, oh *man*,
her dark eyes spill nearly twenty years of bruises,
roll-ups and cider, and a battered Morris van
holds everything she ever wants or uses—
her Dylan tapes, her Steeleye Span and Fleetwood Mac
(he told her once she looked like Stevie Nicks,
and "Go Your Own Way" still takes her back),
her daughter's scribbles, her I-Ching spill-sticks,
the bag of grass hand-picked from her veggie patch,
some tattered old Viragos, Mervyn Peakes
and a book of newish poetry. There's a catch
in her voice as she half-sings, half-speaks
of the slow blues she wrote about him when he left,
that neither of you will remember by the morning
when you have to leave as well and she offers you a lift
through dripping lanes—but it draws you, yawning,
shivering, to huddle in the pile of blankets, quilts
while she clings close, and seems on the edge
of tears; your breath, the frost-blurred ghosts and guilts . . .
We're gonna meet, she tells you, *meet on the ledge.*

ALAN JENKINS

A REPERTOIRE

'Play us one we've never heard before'
we'd ask this old guy in our neighbourhood.
He'd rosin up a good three or four
seconds, stalling, but he always could.
This was the Bronx in 1971,
when every night the sky was pink with arson.
He ran a bar beneath the el, the Blarney Stone,
and there one Easter day he sat us down
and made us tape as much as he could play;
'I gave you these. Make sure you put that down,'
meaning all he didn't have to say.

All that summer we slept on fire escapes,
or tried to sleep, while sirens or the brass
from our neighbour's Tito Puente tapes
kept us up and made us late for mass.
I found our back door bent back to admit
beneath the thick sweet reek of grass
a nest of needles, bottlecaps, and shit.
By August Tom had sold the Blarney Stone
to Puerto Ricans, paid his debts in cash
but left enough to fly his body home.

The bar still rises from the South Bronx ash,
its yellow neon buzzing in the noonday
dark beneath the el, a sheet-steel door
bolted where he played each second Sunday.
'Play me one I've never heard before'
I'd say, and whether he recalled those notes
or made them up, or—since it was Tom who played—
whether it was something in his blood
(cancer, and he was childless and afraid)
I couldn't tell you. And he always would.

MICHAEL DONAGHY

A GENESIS TEXT FOR LARRY LEVIS, WHO DIED ALONE

It will always happen—the death of a friend
That is the beginning of the end of everything
In a large generation of sharing
What was still mistaken
For the nearest middle of all things. So, by extension

I am surely dead, along with David, Phil, Sam,
Marvin, and surely, we all stand
In a succession of etceteras
That is the sentimental, inexhaustible
Exhaustion of most men. It's like

That rainy night of your twenty-eighth birthday.
A strip-joint stuck in the cornfields
Of Coralville, Iowa.
Big teddy bear bikers and pig farmers who were
Not glad to see us: my long hair,
Your azure Hawaiian blouse and David
                        ordering gin—first in blank verse
And then in terza rima with an antique monocle.

The exotic dancer with "helicopter tits," or was
It "tits on stilts," was not coming—a flat on the interstate
From Des Moines her breasts probably sore,
She sat out the storm in the ditch
Feeding white mice to the boa constrictor
Who shared her billing.

So you jumped onto the jukebox and began
A flamenco dance—all the sharp serifs showing a mast,
An erectness that was a happy middle finger
To all those unhappy gentlemen
Seated there in the dark with us.

I walked over to you, looked up—
Begged you to get down before they all
Just simply kicked the shit out of us.
You smiled, sweetly gone.
The song, I think, was called "Pipeline"
And the platform glass of the jukebox cracked.

I said that if you didn't get down
I'd kill you myself. You smiled again
While I aged. I said

The elegy I would write for you would be riddled with clichés!
You giggled.

So now you are dead. Surely, Larry, we've always
Thought the good die young.
And life is a bitch, man.
But where was that woman and her snake when we needed them?

NORMAN DUBIE

SUN-SADDLED, COKE-COPPING, BAD-BOOZING BLUES

Front porch of the first cabin, with Luke.

July, most likely, and damp, both of us wearing rubber boots.

Just out of the photograph, beyond the toe of my left foot,

The railing where Tim and I, one afternoon,

                                     carved our poor initials

While working on verses for his song, "Stockman's Bar Again, Boys."

Both song and singer are gone now, and the railing too.

We all sang in the chorus

                            back in L.A., in the recording studio,

Holly and I and Bill Myers and Kelly and Johnny Rubinstein.

Such joyful music, so long ago,

                         before the coke crash and the whiskey blows.

Sun-soured Montana daydreams,

Los Angeles and its dark snood so soft on the neck.

Lie still I'm working on it lie still.

Billy Mitchell's just come by, somebody stole his tools,

Leland Driggs has shot an elk and broke the county's rules.

Sweet Dan Kelly's on his Cat, watch out and back away,

Snuffy Bruns is feeding squirrels and Crash is bucking hay.

Big John Phelan's got outside a half a fifth of gin,
We've all gone and gotten drunk in Stockman's Bar again.

Dead frequency, Slick, over and out.
It's mostly a matter of what kind of noise you make.
American Hot Wax, for instance, and "Stand by Your Man"—
                              George Jones, type-casting for sure.
And music, always music—keyboard and guitar, violin,
Anything with a string.
                    Your band was called Fun Zone, you up front,
Poncher on drums, Wolfie on bass, and Johnny R. at the piano.

And others. Until the lights went out.
                              Renaissance boy,
With coke up your nose and marijuana in your eye,
We loved you the best we could, but nobody loved you enough.
Except Miss Whiskey.
You roll in your sweet baby's arms now, as once you said you
      would,
And lay your body down,
                    In your meadow, in the mountains, all alone.

TIM MCINTIRE (1944-1986)

CHARLES WRIGHT

GOLDEN OLDIE

I made it home early, only to get
Stalled in the driveway, swaying
At the wheel like a blind pianist caught in a tune
Meant for more than two hands playing.

The words were easy, crooned
By a young girl dying to feel alive, to discover
A pain majestic enough
To live by. I turned the air-conditioning off,

Leaned back to float on a film of sweat,
And listened to her sentiment:
Baby, where did our love go?—a lament
I greedily took in

Without a clue who my lover
Might be, or where to start looking.

RITA DOVE

ENDLESS SLEEP

That was the summer of "Endless Sleep," one of those dopey adolescent
        disaster songs,
electric bass and guitar pounding with an ominous beat, thrumming
        half arythmic
that sounded like a funeral march *ta DUM dum dum dum, ta DUM dum dum dum*
        How my heart
stepped to that gloominess, that solemn procession of morbid notes
        which struck a chord
somehow in my teenage psyche, casting its shadow into every corner of my life.

*

You know the story? Some guy is downcast, desperate because he's argued
        with his girl.
In a transport of sorrow she deserts him, takes a walk one night along the sea,
        all the claptrap
of Gothic romance trundled out to help create a mood of uncertainty
        and fear:
*The night was black / rain fallin' down / looked for my baby / she's nowhere
                around*
        his voice
reverberant, suggesting solitude, some hollowed-out place in the abandoned
        heart.

*

Why did we quarrel / why did we fight / why did I leave her / alone tonight?
        an ecstasy of guilt

I somehow understood, though I can't recall betraying anyone, not then at least,
        still young enough

to believe in the sanctity of love, ravishment unburdened by its flaws,
        perfect love

that harbors a reproach to adults and their lies, their bitter quarrellings—
        if argument

is a form of betrayal, a breach in some ideal of absolute harmony and bliss.

*

Traced her footsteps / down to the shore / 'fraid she's gone /forevermore
        All summer

those dark words pounded my brain, though it seemed a summer more beautiful
        than most,

tall trees billowing with leaves, day after day of immaculate weather.
        I spent hours

fishing from a rock in the middle of the river, transistor radio perched beside me
        blasting

that narrative of Eros and Thanatos over the water crowding me on every side.

I looked at the sea / and it seemed to say / I took your baby / from you away
    What did it mean,

that abyss of water, a single wave reaching out to seize a woman,
    drag her

into depths of cold obliteration that might wash through her to relieve the
       pain?
    Of course

he saves her, plunges in to haul her body from the waves, and so avoids a life
      of misery
    and regret

My heart cried out / she's mine to keep / I saved my baby / from an endless
      sleep.

    *

Who knows what they were arguing about? Each day I pulled fish out of the
      water
    like bright answers,

unable to connect that grave foreboding to the day's abundance,
    its blowing light.

The future spread before me like the surface of the river, beautiful but opaque,
    those lyrics

black as flies dancing in lucid air, while I had visions of a steadfast life,
    a fervent life
free of bitterness and the poison of betrayal. I would never destroy what I loved.

KURT BROWN

HOUSEHOLD GODS

Tuned to 104.6 on the FM
dial, the boom box purrs Golden
Oldies I jerk awake to. You
turn beside me, to me, but turning,
wind tighter into sleep. "I
think it's great," you mumble, each
syllable and breath an array of
totem wrapped in haze—a logo
constructed some finer place than
this, plumb-bob perfect by no
light but the dial's
red rectangle.

Horae Lacrimarum

These hours strung midnight to 7:00's
alarm, each moment a stepping
stone across terrain where music
uncoils and rears to strike, where
wakefulness is goblin, pilgrim,
goblin again. The clutter of eras
packs each moment breathed,
each footprint left, while

Johnny Angel attends your heart like
those household gods Caesar's
Rome raised to block each
portal against barbarian, evil
eye, famine.

              That land you stride through
stretches ahead, behind, buoyed between
lungs, nestled within the rib cage.
For me, it lies as uncharted as
those vast lands cartographers
fixed onto maps millennia ago, pastel
jig-saw pieces they labeled
Terra incognita, and where,
between each vaguely boundaried
blotch, they printed in the best
hand warnings to mariners then, after:
HERE, FRIEND, BE DRAGONS.

JIM ELLEDGE

PHANTOM

It's the last hour of a final day
in June, my wife sleeping,
Bob Dylan going ninety miles an hour
down a dead-end street,
and moments ago—bless the mind
that works against itself—
Hegel conceding that philosophy
always arrives too late.
Through his cat door
here comes our orange cat,
empty-mouthed, looking bereft.
Voles and mice, don't dare relax.
Loners and dreamers, time to test
the dark, visit the haunts.
I'm waiting for that click
of the tape deck or the chapter's end,
whichever comes first—one of those
deals you make with yourself.
It's the click. Now I'll take to bed
this body and the phantom
of what it once was, inseparable
as they are these days, smoke

rising from a stubborn fire.
Night light, be my guide.
I can feel my way just so far.

STEPHEN DUNN

LOVE POTION NO. 9

This is the most beautiful day
Of all time: 80 clear degrees,
Summer sunlight jazzing a slope of trees
Like broccoli against the so-blue sea, boats,

Tiny jewels adrift, silent on the horizon.
From my car parked in front of a church
I can watch the most beautiful boy
I have ever seen mow the lawn: he's blond, maybe 16,

Very tan, skinny, just wearing baggy black shorts,
And all the long young muscles move
Under his warm brown skin
As he shoves the big mower around,

His kid's angel face placid and purposeful. . . .
All the way back along the fast hilly highway
Stands of evergreens and oaks soak up the sun,
The radio blares, I am happy

Thinking of the boy and the sea. Racing

The twist of roads home, the beautiful gargle
Of twin camshafts at 4000 rpm tells me
That this is all I need: 5 P.M. melon-colored sunlight

Slanting over the silver hood. What greens
In the trees, what a rich cerulean sky, what joy
Kicking it down into third
And screaming around the curve,

Soundgarden on the radio, and the retinal image
Of the grass-mowing kid even better than Tiepolo,
Better than Brahms, reachable, ecstatic, true.
O this is the world I want without end.

ROBERT LONG

PARKERSBURG

I will arise now and put on a black baseball cap and go
to Parkersburg. It will fit me,
the cap will, and it will be black,
the sneakers on my feet will be purple,
and I will not have shaved for three days.
The day will be rainy and cool
and I will wear an old jacket of pale wool
that was once my Uncle Lew's,
and go to Parkersburg.

On a bus I may go
or in an old car full of tapes—
Elmore James. Fred McDowell.
The Kinks. Into the town of Parkersburg
on a day so rainy and cool. And I will be
terrifically untroubled if anyone thinks I am strange,
in fact everything about this day will be a ratification
of how I am not them; and my manner, though courteous,
will tend to make them suspect that they are boring.
They will wonder why they have no purple sneakers. Cool

and lightly rainy in Parkersburg
and me all day there exactly as if my belief
had long been firm; not forgetting for one minute
how I felt listening to "I'm Different" by Randy Newman
years ago and the sacred tears in my eyes at that time.
I and my black baseball cap will enter a tavern

and there we will read a French poet with such concentration
it will be like I *am* that guy. Then pretty soon
in another tavern it is a Spanish poet whom I read
with similar effect. Parkersburg!
Oh my Parkersburg . . . And I swear,
though I might not meet a lonely marvelous slim woman
with black hair, it will still be as if I did.

MARK HALLIDAY

ELVIS'S TWIN SISTER

ARE YOU LONESOME TONIGHT? DO YOU MISS ME TONIGHT?

ELVIS IS ALIVE AND SHE'S FEMALE.

—*MADONNA*

In the convent, y'all,
I tend the gardens,
watch things grow,
pray for the immortal soul
of rock 'n' roll.

They call me
Sister Presley here.
The Reverend Mother
digs the way I move my hips
just like my brother.

Gregorian chant
drifts out across the herbs,
Pascha nostrum immolatus est . . .
I wear a simple habit,
darkish hues,

a wimple with a novice-sewn
lace band, a rosary,
a chain of keys,
a pair of good and sturdy
blue suede shoes.

I think of it
as Graceland here,
a land of grace.
It puts my trademark slow lopsided smile
back on my face.

Lawdy.
I'm alive and well.
Long time since I walked
down Lonely Street
towards Heartbreak Hotel.

CAROL ANN DUFFY

ELVIS PRESLEY

Two minutes long it pitches through some bar:
Unreeling from a corner box, the sigh
Of this one, in his gangling finery
And crawling sideburns, wielding a guitar.

The limitations where he found success
Are ground on which he, panting, stretches out
In turn, promiscuously, by every note.
Our idiosyncrasy and our likeness.

We keep ourselves in touch with a mere dime:
Distorting hackneyed words in hackneyed songs
He turns revolt into a style, prolongs
The impulse to a habit of the time.

Whether he poses or is real, no cat
Bothers to say: the pose held is a stance,
Which, generation of the very chance
It wars on, may be posture for combat.

THOM GUNN

THE WINE TALKS

Evelyn Rankin and I were having dinner
at Montecito's, the best and most expensive
restaurant in town, to celebrate the completion
of a big project at work. To help wash down
the fabulous foods we had ordered some very
fine wines. Finally, after hours of great
fun, I asked for the bill. The owner himself
came to our table. "You are a beautiful
couple," he said with a warm smile. "How
long have you been married?" "Twenty-five
years," I said. "We are celebrating our
anniversary tonight in your lovely restaurant,"
I said. "You seem so happy, so much in love
still. Please, let this evening be on me.
It brings me joy to serve such a happy couple."
"Oh, no, we couldn't," Evelyn protested.
"I insist," he said. "Thank you so much,"
I said, standing to shake his hand. I drove
Evelyn home in silence. I walked her to her
door. I had never even thought of kissing
her before. "We made him happy," I said.

"Is that so bad?" "Do you think we could have lasted twenty-five years?" she asked. "Evelyn," I said, "it's been a perfectly lovely evening, and now it's over." I leaned toward her and kissed her lightly on the lips, turned and said good night. For all I know she may have a giant tattoo of Elvis on her back.

JAMES TATE

THE SUN SESSIONS

AFTER OTIS BLACKWELL

'56.
Amphibious,
barely out of his tail.

Heart in his mouth. Don't.
Perhaps he is trying
to swallow it.

The bull-frogs on backing
inflate. Be true. Oo oo oo.
On the tough acoustic

of an empty pool. Don't.
To a heart. Doo wah.
That's cruel. Sha la la la.

De dum. I mean
cruel. Wo wo wo wo.
And true.

LAVINIA GREENLAW

SHORE LEAVE

She wears the sailor suit—a blouse with anchors,
skirt puffed in stiff tiers above her thin
knees, those spit-shined party shoes. Behind her
a Cadillac's fabulous fins gleam and reflected
in the showroom window, her father's a mirage.
The camera blocks his face as he frames
a shot that freezes her serious grin,
the splendid awkwardness of almost-adolescence.
He's all charm with the car dealer and fast-talks
them a test-drive in a convertible like the one
on display, a two-tone Coupe de Ville. But once
around the corner he lowers the top and soon
they're fishtailing down dump-truck paths,
the Jersey meadows smoldering with trash fires.
He's shouting *Maybelline, why can't you be true*,
and seagulls lift in a tattered curtain across
Manhattan's hazy skyline. Dust-yellow clouds
behind him, he's handsome as a matinee idol,
wavy hair blown straight by sheer velocity.
Tall marshweeds bend, radiant as her heart's
relentless tide. They rip past gaping Frigidaires,
rusted hulks of cranes abandoned to the weather.

Her father teases her she's getting so pretty
he'll have to jump ship sometime and take her
on a real whirl, maybe paint the whole town red.
For her *merchant marine* conjures names like
condiments—Malabar, Marseilles—places where
the laws of gravity don't hold. She can't believe
her father's breakneck luck will ever run out.
He accelerates and spins out as if the next thrill
will break through to some more durable joy.
So she stands, hands atop the windshield and shouts
the chorus with him, and later when they drop the car
he takes her to a cocktail bar and plays Chuck Berry
on the juke box. She perches on a bar stool and twirls
her Shirley Temple's paper umbrella, watches
the slick vinyl disks stack up, rhythms collecting,
breaking like surf as her father asks the barmaid
to dance with him through "Blue Moon," then foamy
glass after glass of beer. The barmaid's sinuous
in red taffeta, a rhinestone choker around
her throat. Her father's forgotten her and dances
a slow, slow tango in the empty bar and the dark
comes on like the tiny black rose on the barmaid's
shoulder rippling under her father's hand.

The girl thinks someday she'll cover her skin
with roses, then spins, dizzy on the bar stool.
She doesn't hear the woman call her foolish
mortal father a two-bit trick because she's whirling
until the room's a band of light continuous
with the light the city's glittering showrooms throw
all night long over the sleek, impossible cars.

LYNDA HULL

CHER

I wanted to be Cher, tall
as a glass of iced tea,
her bony shoulders draped
with a curtain of dark hair
that plunged straight down,
the cut tips brushing
her non-existent butt.
I wanted to wear a lantern
for a hat, a cabbage, a piñata
and walk in six-inch heels that buttoned
up the back. I wanted her
rouged cheekbones and her
throaty panache, her voice
of gravel and clover, the hokum
of her clothes: black fishnet
and pink pom-poms, frilled
halter tops, fringed bells
and that thin strip of waist
with the bullet hole navel.
Cher standing with her skinny arm
slung around Sonny's thick neck,
posing in front of the Eiffel Tower,
The Leaning Tower of Pisa,

The Great Wall of China,
The Crumbling Pyramids, smiling
for the camera with her crooked
teeth, hit-and-miss beauty, the sun
bouncing off the bump on her nose.
Give me back the old Cher,
the gangly, imperfect girl
before the shaving knife
took her, before they put
pillows in her tits, injected
the lumpy gel into her lips.
Take me back to the woman
I wanted to be, stalwart
and silly, smart as her lion
tamer's whip, my body a torch
stretched along the length
of the polished piano, legs
bent at the knee, hair cascading
down over Sonny's blunt fingers
as he pummeled the keys,
singing in a sloppy alto
the oldest, saddest songs.

DORIANNE LAUX

CHIFFON

Fever, down-right dirty sweat
    of a heat-wave in May turning everyone
        pure body. Back of knee, cleavage, each hidden

crease, nape of neck turning steam. Deep
    in last night's vast factory, the secret
        wheels that crank the blue machinery

of weather bestowed this sudden cool,
    the lake misting my morning walk, this
        vacant lot lavish with iris—saffron,

indigo, bearded and striated, a shock
    of lavender clouds among shattered brick
        like cumulus that sail the tops of highrises

clear evenings. Surprising as the iris garden
    I used to linger in, a girl distant from me
        now as a figure caught in green glass,

an oasis gleamed cool with oval plaques
    naming blooms Antoinette, My Blue Sunset,
        Festival Queen. This morning's iris frill

damp as fabulous gowns after dancing,
    those rummage sale evening gowns church ladies
        gave us another hot spring, 1967.

JoAnn who'd soon leave school, 14, pregnant,
    Valerie with her straightened bouffant hair.
        That endless rooftop season before the panic

and sizzle, the torched divided cities,
    they called me *cousin on the light side.*
        Camphorous, awash in rusty satin rosettes,

in organdy, chiffon, we'd practice
    girl group radio-hits—Martha Reeves
        but especially Supremes—JoAnn vamping

Diana, me and Valerie doing Flo and Mary's
    background moans, my blonde hair pinned
        beneath Jo's mother's Sunday wig.

The barest blue essence of Evening in Paris
    scented our arms. We perfected all the gestures,
        JoAnn's liquid hands sculpting air,

her fingers' graceful cupping, wrist turning,
    palm held flat, "Stop in the Name of Love,"
        pressing against the sky's livid contrails,

a landscape flagged with laundry, tangled
    aerials and billboards, the blackened
        railway bridges and factories ruinous

in their fumes. Small hand held against the flood
    of everything to come, the savage drifting years.
        I'm a lucky bitch. Engulfed in the decade's riotous

swells, that lovely gesture, the dress, plumage
    electrifying the fluid force of that young body.
        She was gang-raped later that year. The rest,

as they say is *history*. History.
    When I go back I pore the phone book for names
        I'll never call. Peach Pavilion, Amethyst

Surprise. *Cousin on the light side.* Bend
   to these irises, their piercing ambrosial
      essence, the heart surprised, dark and bitter.

LYNDA HULL

ANNUS MIRABILIS

Sexual intercourse began
In nineteen sixty-three
(which was rather late for me)—
Between the end of the "Chatterley" ban
And the Beatles' first LP.

Up to then there'd only been
A sort of bargaining,
A wrangle for the ring,
A shame that started at sixteen
And spread to everything.

Then all at once the quarrel sank:
Everyone felt the same,
And every life became
A brilliant breaking of the bank,
A quite unlosable game.

So life was never better than
In nineteen sixty-three
(Though just too late for me)—

Between the end of the "Chatterley" ban
and the Beatles' first LP.

PHILIP LARKIN

THE ASSASSINATION OF JOHN LENNON
AS DEPICTED BY THE MADAME TUSSAUD
WAX MUSEUM, NIAGARA FALLS, ONTARIO, 1987

Smuggled human hair from Mexico
Falls radiant around the waxy O

Of her scream. Shades on, leather coat and pants, Yoko
On her knees—like the famous Kent State photo

Where the girl can't shriek her boyfriend alive, her arms
Windmilling Ohio sky.

                              A pump in John's chest heaves

To mimic death throes. The blood is made of latex.
His glasses: broken on the plastic sidewalk.

A scowling David Chapman, his arms outstretched,
His pistol barrel spiraling fake smoke

In a siren's red wash, completes the composition,
And somewhere background music plays "Imagine"

Before the tableau darkens. We push a button
To renew the scream.

                        The chest starts up again.

DAVID WOJAHN

YEAH YEAH YEAH

No matter what you did to her, she said,

There's times, she said, she misses you, your face

Will pucker in her dream, and times the bed's

Too big. Stray hairs will surface in a place

You used to leave your shoes. A certain phrase,

Some old song on the radio, a joke

You had to be there for, she said, some days

It really gets to her; the way you smoked

Or held a cup, or her, and how you woke

Up crying in the night sometimes, the way

She'd stroke and hush you back, and how you broke

Her still. All this she told me yesterday,

Then she rolled over, laughed, began to do

To me what she so rarely did with you.

RODDY LUMSDEN

FROM ME TO YOU

Dear Yoko,

Do you want to know a secret?
I was a fool on a hill till there was you. I was crippled inside.
It took a long, long, long time and now I'm so happy I found you.
Love, don't ever change.

On this sleepless night, imagine yesterday, like dreamers do.
He thought that happiness was a warm gun.
Forgive me, my little flower princess.
I just had a ticket to ride. Let it be.

Here comes the sun, and golden slumbers fill my eyes.
I've got a feeling it won't be long until the two of us come together
And live in strawberry fields forever.

Tell our beautiful boy, our darling boy, that I feel fine.

Oh Yoko, oh my love. One day at a time.
Remember, yes, I'm your angel.

All my loving across the universe.

John

P.S. I love you—here, there, and everywhere

ROBYN FIALKOW

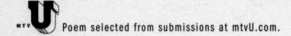 Poem selected from submissions at mtvU.com.

BED MUSIC

Our love was new,
But your bedsprings were old.
In the flat below,
They stopped eating
With forks in the air.

They made the old sourpuss
Climb the stairs
And squint through the keyhole,
While we went right ahead
Making the springs toot,

Playing "Low Down on the Bayou,"
Playing "Big Leg Mama,"
Playing "Shake It Baby"
And "Carolina Shout."

That was the limit!
They called the fire brigade.
They called the Law.
They could've brought some hooch,
We told the cops.

CHARLES SIMIC

ROCK MUSIC

The ocean glittered quietly in the moonlight
While heavy metal rocked the discotheques;
Space-age Hondas gurgled half the night,
Fired by the prospect of fortuitous sex.
I sat late at the window, blind with rage,
And listened to the tumult down below,
Trying to concentrate on the printed page
As if such obsolete bumph could save us now.

(Frank Ifield, Clodagh Rodgers, where are you now?
Every night by the window here I sit.
Sandie and Bobby, I still remember you—
As for the Arcadia, though I remember it,
It no longer remembers the uncouth Coke-heads
Who trembled here in nineteen fifty-six
In ice-cream parlours and amusement arcades;
Oddities all, we knew none of the tricks.

Cinema organ, easy listening, swing, doowop, bebop,
Sedate me with your subliminal sublime
And give me that old trashy '50s pop,

Suburban burblings of an earlier time;
The boogie bins bouncing in rotary light,
Give me my toxic shame, mean woman blues,
That old self-pity where, lonesome tonight,
I sit here snarling in my blue suede shoes.)

Next morning, wandering on the strand, I heard
Left-over echoes of the night before
Dwindle to echoes, and a single bird
Drown with a whistle that residual roar.
Rock music started up on every side—
Whisper of algae, click of stone on stone,
A thousand limpets left by the ebb-tide
Unanimous in their silent inquisition.

DEREK MAHON

NORTH(WEST)ERN

I was twelve as in the 12-bar blues, sick
for the Southeast, marooned on the North Wales coast,
a crotchet, my tongue craving the music
of Welsh, Scouse or Manc: entering the outpost

of Colwyn Bay Pier, midsummer, noon,
niteclub for those of us with the deep ache
of adolescence, when I heard that tune.
Named it in one. Soul. My heart was break

dancing on the road to Wigan Casino,
Northern Soul mecca, where transatlantic bass
beat blacker than blue in glittering mono

then back via Southport, Rhyl to the time, place
I bit the Big Apple. Black. Impatient. Young.
A string of pips exploding on my tongue.

PATIENCE AGBABI

SOME CRAZY DANCING

I think I must have spent great chunks of those years
watching the girls and boys on American Bandstand,
the frug and boogaloo shaking through their furious bodies.
I stood by the TV and danced along. I wish
I could say I was another girl, that my stories were those
of the girl who walked off-set, leading a boy—his license
snug in a back pocket—into shadow. I wish I could say
I was the girl who knew what to do with her tongue.
What I wanted in those years was mostly everything:
the neatly belted torsos, the girl's high tits,
all the worn places on the guy's jeans.
What I wanted was not to have to do one thing.
And in front of that TV as I shimmied, ponied and posed,
one afternoon I heard a man's voice somewhere close by saying
—and this I remember exactly—*Fuck me, fuck baby, do me.*
Of course the voice was inside me. Not hard to imagine why,
but harder to imagine how my own indecency undid me.
I flipped the channel, then shut it off and went out
into a nest of suburban streets; walking past landscaped
lawns, shaped bushes, cut-back flowering trees, the slate
front walks up to doors where anyone might emerge.
I know I believed it was finite:

the universe of sex moving inside me,

stars burning out, streaking through the sky, and me—

too afraid to look up or down. Under a neighbor's dogwood,

under the excitement of petals, I waited for that

insistent voice inside to step out and show me what was what.

I can't help it, it seems sweet now—desire—

can I even call it that?—more a demand,

like Dick Clark calling out some latest dance craze,

some new-fangled routine that you'd believe

might be the season's best.

VICTORIA REDEL

DISCO ELEGY

FOR VINNY SAVARESE, 1958-1976

You were barely old enough to drive
And gave your pulsing body to the beat.
All you wanted was to stay alive,

To let the primal rhythm's pounding tide
Wash over you and guide your flagrant feet.
You were barely old enough to drive

To "Fifty-Four," "2001"—sexual hives
Throbbing through the night, those bodies
Sweating, passionate to stay alive.

A stud in heels and chains, hair blow-dried,
You strutted like Travolta down the street,
A cock of the walk on overdrive;

And did The Hustle, The Bump and Grind,
The dance floor pumping with collective heat
Under a flashing ball—Stayin' Alive!

O it was kitsch, but who wouldn't reprise
Innocence awash in its churning sea,
Those first days of being old enough to drive.
All you wanted was to stay alive.

DANIEL TOBIN

I LIKE THE MUSIC THAT SHAKES

In the courtyard of the asylum retarded men
counted out a new mountain of plastic strips
each day, color by color, the remains of
one distant celebration refurbished for the next.
Their bodies were sewing machines set at different speeds,
seizures of tics and unheard rhythms.

Ashamed of my promise I waved to them from a distance,
me between the orderly oak trees of my school
and them behind stucco walls, the filigree gate.
A man waved back, hand and trunk and eye
disjointed and obtuse.

When I entered my room that afternoon
and saw him hunched over the turntable, lifting
the needle and setting it down in a different groove
of music, dancing some liquid steps in his black
butcher's shoes to Emerson's strobelike organ
he spotted me and said, one cow eye open,
"I like the music that shakes."

And who would question the chance for that body
to be free of its episodes, ritual and intense,
to slip through its caging in another rhythm's grip
and skate like an escaped quarter across the parquet
floor toward its measureless future?

JONATHAN WELLS

DELIVERING EGGS TO THE GIRLS' DORM

I AM THE EGG MAN . . .

—*JOHN LENNON*

For me it was the cherry blossoms flooding
Olive Sreet and softening the dawn,
the windows flung open in a yawn,
billowing curtains pregnant with the breeze,
the sounds of Procol Harum entering the air,
and fifty girls rising in their underwear.

O lost love. My girl and I had just split up.
The leaves of chestnut trees were rinsed in black,
the wind moaned grief, the moon was on the rack.
Humped over, stacking egg-crates in my Ford,
I was Charles Laughton ringing bells at Notre Dame—
spurned, wounded, but still in love with Sheila Baum.

Arriving at the gates of paradise,
I rang the service bell to wait on
Mrs. Cornish in her saintly apron
fumbling at the door, and the raucous gush

of female voices when she opened it. The flour
in her beard announced the darkness of the hour:

You're late. The hiss of bacon, pancake batter
as it kissed the grill, were a swarm of snakes to warn
the innocent away. Inside were virgins born,
like Sheila Baum, to stay that way. Outside
stood the egg man, despairing in his oval fate:
fifty girls staring, eggless, at an empty plate.

They may still be staring there. For emptiness
became my theme, sweeping eggshells
from my car, driving empty streets, fall's
cherry trees as bare as dormitory walls
washed by September rains. And the bells of Notre Dame
were as still as the broken shell of my dream of Sheila Baum.

B. H. FAIRCHILD

AN ENGLISHMAN ABROAD

(FOR CHRISTOPHER LOGUE)

The talk-radio host is trying to shake the wacko
with only a minute left
to get in the finance and boner-pill spots
before signing off,
the morning news team already at the door
and dairy vans streaming
from the gates of WholesomeBest, fanning out
across the vast plateau.
Fair skies, high cumulus cloud—
the birds are in full throat as dawn ignites
in the east, rinsing the heavens with a coral pink.

What power and wealth,
the foreign visitor reflects from his bed
in the quaint, *old west* hotel,
two military jets thundering by overhead.
He takes in the embroidered homilies on the walls,
the highboy and phony Windsor chairs,
and begins to smell the coffee and bacon
frying down the stairs. He is not at all ready

to say good-bye
to this resourceful, generous, open-faced tribe
with its matchless plumbing and inexhaustible vistas.

To the west, prevailing winds
deposit a vapor of phenols, benzene, sulfides
across the grasslands, choking back
the cinquefoil and flowering tansy,
slowly dismantling the proteins in the curlew's bill.
He remembers the pretty blond attendant
at the laundrette, her shy but persistent
queries about his accent and native Portsmouth,
and that lingering smile.
Angel food cake   *black camisole*
          Voucheron   *spike heels:*
revery, tumescence, gladness—when just then

the clock radio comes on
with its farm report followed by an ancient Procol Harum tune
that takes him uncomfortably back, way back
to a calamitous party in Shepherd's Bush.
What a hateful dismal shitty little village
London really is.

Should he have pursued her? In earnest?
She seemed keen enough at the time
but these amorous gambits of late
have one after another come a cropper.
One tires of being made to feel the fool.

They gave him everything, these good people
A magnificent stage, first-rate lighting
and packed houses every night.
They'd have wept real tears on the West End to see it.
And *here*, in the middle of blinking nowhere.
Just look at the color of those clouds.
Rosy-fingered dawn, my ass.
This show's in Technicolor.
The telephone. Must be his minder.
—*Yes, yes, I'll be ready downstairs at 8.*
Excellent girl. I should remember
to send her a little something when I get back.
Toffee or some silly English thing or other.

They can't get enough of all that, poor dears.
What was that joke the department Chair told?
No matter. A most amusing chap.

You don't suppose it will be another of those
awful little commuter jets?
I'll be shattered by the time I get to Denver,
much less Heathrow.
What was that darling girl's name?
Jeanie, Janie, Joanie. Jeanine. *Jeanette*.
Yes, that was it. Lovely creature.
Why do I scruple so?
It's an affliction, that's what it is.
Bloody hell . . .

AUGUST KLEINZAHLER

HANOI HANNAH

Ray Charles! His voice
calls from waist-high grass,
& we duck behind gray sandbags.
"Hello, Soul Brothers. Yeah,
Georgia's also on my mind."
Flares bloom over the trees.
"Here's Hannah again.
Let's see if we can't
light her goddamn fuse
this time." Artillery
shells carve a white arc
against dusk. Her voice rises
from a hedgerow on our left.
"It's Saturday night in the States.
Guess what your woman's doing tonight.
I think I'll let Tina Turner
Tell you, you homesick GIs."
Howitzers buck like a herd
of horses behind concertina.
"You know you're dead men,
don't you? You're dead

as King today in Memphis.
Boys, you're surrounded by
General Tran Do's division."
Her knife-edge song cuts
deep as a sniper's bullet.
"Soul Brothers, what are you dying for?"
We lay down a white-klieg
trail of tracers. Phantom jets
fan out over the trees.
Artillery fire zeros in.
Her voice grows flesh
& we can see her falling
into words, a bleeding flower
no one knows the true name for.
"You're lousy shots, GIs."
Her laughter floats up
as though the airways are
buried under our feet.

YUSEF KOMUNYAKAA

OOLY POOP A COW

My brother Charles
brought home the news
the kids were saying
take a flying leap
and eat me raw
and be bop a lula.

Forty miles he rode
the bus there and back.
The dog and I met him
at the door, panting
for hoke poke, hoke
de waddy waddy hoke poke.

In Cu Chi, Vietnam,
I heard tapes somebody's
sister sent of wild thing,
I think I love you
and hey now, what's that
sound, everybody look what's . . .

Now it's my daughters
bringing home no-duh,
rock out, whatever,
like I totally
paused, and like
I'm like . . .

I'm like Mother, her hands
in biscuit dough,
her ears turning red
from ain' nothing butta,
blue Monday, and
tutti fruiti, aw rooty!

DAVID HUDDLE

SLEEP, AFTER RAY CHARLES SHOW AND HURRICANE REPORT

A storm named for a woman
was born as a mild
disturbance off Africa.
It broke into interiors

of pianos, blew the tubes
of trees and went on
record with weed for its whistle.
Now, bystanding, I

come down with a blessed
attack of the dance. I am white
trash, brother, one more basket
case. You boss the winds

like nobody's business, but nobody
can bear or see himself.
Life is the mother
with murder in her eye, and we

are junked and treasured,
every one regardless.

HEATHER MCHUGH

SLEEVE NOTES

MICK JAGGER: *ROCK MUSIC WAS A COMPLETELY NEW MUSICAL FORM. IT HADN'T BEEN AROUND FOR TEN YEARS WHEN WE STARTED DOING IT. NOW IT'S FORTY YEARS OLD.*
JANN S. WENNER: *WHAT ABOUT YOUR OWN STAYING POWER?*
MICK JAGGER: *I HAVE A LOT OF ENERGY, SO I DON'T SEE IT AS AN IMMEDIATE PROBLEM.*
JANN S. WENNER: *HOW'S YOUR HEARING?*
MICK JAGGER: *MY HEARING'S ALL RIGHT. SOMETIMES I USE EARPLUGS BECAUSE IT GETS TOO LOUD ON MY LEFT EAR.*
JANN S. WENNER: *WHY YOUR LEFT EAR?*
MICK JAGGER: *BECAUSE KEITH'S STANDING ON MY LEFT.*

"JAGGER REMEMBERS," ROLLING STONE, *MARCH 1996*

THE JIMI HENDRIX EXPERIENCE: *Are You Experienced?*

"Like being driven over by a truck"
was how Pete Townshend described the effect
of the wah-wah on "I Don't Live Today."

This predated by some months the pedal
Clapton used on "Tales of Brave Ulysses"
And I'm taken aback (jolt upon jolt)
to think that Hendrix did it all "by hand."

To think, moreover, that he used *four*-track

one-inch tape has (jolt upon jolt) evoked
the long, long view from the Senior Study
through the smoke, yes sir, the smoke of battle
on the fields of Laois, yes sir, and Laos.

Then there was the wah-wah on "Voodoo Child
(Slight Return)" from *Electric Ladyland.*

CREAM: *Disreali Gears*

As I labored over the "Georgiks and Bukolikis"
I soon learned to tell thunder from dynamite.

THE BEATLES: *The Beatles*

Though that was the winter when late each night
I'd put away Cicero or Caesar
and pour new milk into an old saucer
for the hedgehog which, when it showed up right
on cue, would set its nose down like that flight
back from the U.S. . . . back from the, yes sir
back from the . . . back from the U.S.S.R. . . .
I'd never noticed the play on "*album*" and "*white.*"

THE ROLLING STONES: *Beggar's Banquet*

Thanks to Miss Latimore,
I was "coming along nicely" at piano

while, compared to the whoops and wild halloos
of the local urchins,

my diction
was im-pecc-a-ble.

In next to no time I would be lost
to the milk bars

and luncheonettes
of smoky Belfast,

where a troubadour
such as the frontman of Them

had long since traded in the lute
for bass and blues harmonica.

VAN MORRISON: *Astral Weeks*

Not only had I lived on Fitzroy Avenue,
I'd lived there with Madame Georgie Hyde Lees,
to whom I would rather shortly be wed.

Georgie would lose out to The George and El Vino's
when I "ran away to the BBC"
as poets did, so Dylan Thomas said.

ERIC CLAPTON: *461 Ocean Boulevard*

It's the house in all its whited sepulchritude
(not the palm tree against which dogs piddle
as they make their way back from wherever
it was they were all night) that's really at a list.

Through the open shutters his music, scatty, skewed,
skids and skites from the neck of a bottle
that might turn on him, might turn and sever
an artery, the big one that runs through his wrist.

ELVIS COSTELLO AND THE ATTRACTIONS: *My Aim Is True*

Even the *reductio ad absurdum*
of the *quid pro quo* or "tit for tat"
killing (For "Eilis" read "Alison")

that now took over from the street riot
was not without an old-fashioned
sense of decorum, an unseemly seemliness.

WARREN ZEVON: *Excitable Boy*

Somewhere between *Ocean Boulevard* and *Slowhand*
I seemed to have misplaced my wedding band
and then taken up with waitresses and usherettes
who drank straight gins and smoked crooked cheroots.

Since those were still the days when more meant less
Georgie was herself playing fast and loose
with the werewolf who, not so very long before,
had come how-howling round our kitchen door

and introduced me to Warren Zevon, whose hymns

to booty, to beasts, to bimbos, boom boom,
are inextricably part of the warp and woof
of the wild and wicked poems in *Quoof*.

DIRE STRAITS: *Dire Straits*

There was that time the archangel ran his thumb along the shelf
and anointed, it seemed, his own brow with soot.

BLONDIE: *Parallel Lines*

It had taken all morning to rehearse
a tracking shot

with an Arriflex
mounted on a gurney.

The dream of rain
on the face of a well.

"Ready when you are, Mr. DeMilledoon."
Another small crowd

on the horizon.
We should have rented a Steadicam.

BRUCE SPRINGSTEEN: *The River*

So it was I gave up the Oona for the Susquehanna,
the Shannon for the Shenandoah.

LLOYD COLE AND THE COMMOTIONS: *Easy Pieces*

Though not before I'd done my stint on the Cam.
The ceilings taller than the horizon.

The in-crowd
on the outs with the likes of Milton

and Spenser while Cromwell
still walked through the pouring rain.

In graveyards from Urney
to Ardglass, my countrymen laying down some *Lex*

talionis: "Only the guy who's shot
gets to ride in the back of the hearse."

TALKING HEADS: *True Stories*

You can take the man out of Armagh but, you may ask yourself,
can you take the Armagh out of the man in the big Armani suit?

U2: *The Joshua Tree*

When I went to hear them in Giants Stadium
a year or two ago, the whiff
of kef
brought back the night we drove all night from Palm

Springs to Blythe. No Irish lad and his lass
were so happy as we who roared
and soared
through yucca-scented air. Dawn brought a sense of loss,

faint at first, that would deepen and expand
as our own golden chariot
was showered
with Zippo spears from the upper tiers of the stands.

PINK FLOYD: *A Momentary Lapse of Reason*

We stopped in at a roadhouse on the way back from Lyonesse
and ordered a Tom Collins and an Old-Fashioned.
As we remounted the chariot

the poplar's synthesized alamo-alamo-eleison
was counterpointed by a redheaded woodpecker's rat-tat-tat
on a snare, a kettledrum's de dum de dum.

PAUL SIMON: *Negotiations and Love Songs*

Little did I think as I knelt by a pothole
to water my elephant with the other elephant drivers,
little did I think as I chewed on some betel

that I might one day be following the river
down the West Side Highway in his smoke-glassed
limo complete with bodyguard-cum-chauffeur

and telling him that his lyrics must surely last:
little did I think as I chewed and chewed
that my own teeth and tongue would be eaten by rust.

LEONARD COHEN: *I'm Your Man*

When I turn up the rickety old gramophone
the wow and flutter from a scratched LP
summons up white walls, the table, the single bed

where Lydia Languish will meet her Le Fanu:
his songs have meant far more to me
than most of the so-called poems I've read.

NIRVANA: *Bleach*

I went there, too, with Mona, or Monica.
Another shot of Absolut.

"The Wild Rover" or some folk anthem
on the jukebox. Some dour

bartender. I, too, have been held fast
by those snares and nets

off the Zinc Coast, the coast of Zanzibar,
                              lost
              able

addiction

"chin-chins"

loos,

"And it's no,
nay, never, no nay never no more . . ."

BOB DYLAN: *Oh Mercy*

All great artists are their own greatest threat,
as when they aim an industrial laser
at themselves and cut themselves back to the root

so that, with spring, we can never ever be sure
if they shake from head to foot
from an orgasm, you see, sir, or a seizure.

R.E.M.: *Automatic for the People*

Like the grasping for air by an almighty mite
who's suffering from a bad case of the colic.

THE ROLLING STONES: *Voodoo Lounge*

Giants Stadium again . . . Again the scent of drugs
struggling through rain so heavy some young Turks
would feel obliged to butt-hole
surf across those vast puddles

on the field. Some might have burned damp faggots
on a night like this, others faked
the ho-ho-hosannas and the hallelujahs
with their *"Tout passé, tout casse, tout lasse."*

The Stones, of course, have always found the way
of setting a burning brand
to a petrol-soaked stack of hay

and making a "Thou Shalt"
of a "Thou Shalt Not." The sky over the Meadowlands
was still aglow as I drove home to my wife and child.

PAUL MULDOON

THE BURNING OF THE MIDNIGHT LAMP

Listening to *Purple Haze* and *The Wind Cries Mary*,
Let Me Stand Next to Your Fire and *Manic Depression*,

I am drifting undersea toward strobe lights
and feedback, the dreamy, acoustic waves of 1969.

Remember how you explained those dirty sounds—
the two-note riff banned by the Spanish Inquisition,

the hammer-ons and pull-offs, the sharpened ninth?
Is it tomorrow or just the end of time?

I've forgotten nothing. Any moment I'll cross
the campus near the dormitory where you've moved in

with another man; I'll pause under the window trembling
with volume—a betrayer betrayed and turning back

to the raw, metallic, bristling taste of wind.
The morning is dead and the day is too

There's nothing left here to lead me, but the velvet moon
(you always liked the wah-wah pedal on that song).

...

Someone is playing *Voodoo Child* and *House Burning Down*,
checking the chord progression in *Spanish Castle Magic*

and the octaves in *Third Stone from the Sun*.
another is blasting *Crosstown Traffic* from a lounge

where darkness branches into maroon rivers
and cigarette butts flare into the stars.

No more parties with our friends eating seeds
and lacing punch, smoking joints in a dim room

where you go on talking about sinister bent strings
and dive-bombing sounds, the devil invoked

in the interval of a tritone or flattened fifth.
No more waiting for you to return to me

(that forgotten earring lying on the floor)
through a downpour of left-handed notes.

But sometimes when I close my eyes
I see your body fading back into shadows.

                    ...

As a child, Jimi Hendrix watched his soul floating
away from his torso, looking down at himself

from a different realm. He was awake but slipping
mindlessly through another dimension, the astral plane.

That's how you felt about LSD and STP,
those ten-milligram doses of the sublime.

We were looking for fire escapes: ladders
and watchtowers spiraling up from the ground.

But that year as I smoldered within my body
and you tripped through the acid nights

Orpheus stomped microphones and humped speakers,
smashing amplifiers on stage after stage

as though he could whammy the Underworld
into submission and subdue the Furies

while darkness vibrated around him
and electric guitars exploded in flames.

EDWARD HIRSCH

ELECTRIC CHURCH

I EITHER PLAY VERY VERY SOFT OR VERY VERY LOUD.

—JIMI HENDRIX

Peace and love are shit but I believe

no napalm fell out of the American heavens,

                                no cities burned

            when Johnie Allen

        Hendricks

            burned his Strat at Monterrey.

            No demons

                        were in the neighborhood—

    when that fey spring of the Summer of Love

        went up in lighter-fluid smoke

and the final buzz-saw grace note

                    fed the sweet

                        leaping flames,

            something other

    than Armageddon happened,

                        than mere hallucinogens.

        It was as if the roar of those killed dead

                        would never stop

and that last subway rush of feedback

was not apocalypse

but animal memory,

a full sustain of consciousness

freaked

to keening,

smoke that never burns

making its way in time—

it lasts. It exceeds

the strictest ember.

It wastes its little heat

while the heart, breaking on

and on,

merely is,

and loss is everything else

and what this means,

already over,

is just beginning.

Someone said that somewhere into the murderous

suspended bridge of "Wild Thing"

he bore his Strat

above his head

and the damned thing

                                        played without him

and gasped like someone crying

                              as this someone's country dies

                and dies.

                              Years of idolatrous viewings and I

    believe

that he was not a Voodoo Child

                    but some motherless family's

                    little man,

                              to whom the feedback sounded

                                        as a big plane had

                    lumbering through Georgia skies

                    to an enlistee parachutist,

                                        a Screaming Eagle,

                                        throwing open

                the cabin door—

                              falling away from the sound

                              of a howling machine

        down towards a quiet airforce base,

                                        its thousand Quonset

    huts

                a regiment of endless mailboxes,

                              its airfield

              of silenced moths . . .

                                    and the surrounding farms,

           red roads and everyday casualties—

                          the one, unbroken,

                                    rising

                                    deafening world.

WILLIAM OLSEN

ALL ALONG THE WATCHTOWER

I remember the pink, candy-colored lights
strung around an auditorium
shaped like an enormous ear
and a single, distant figure on a stage, gripping a guitar
that twisted like a serpent

trying to turn into a bird.
Sixteen, high on acid for the first time,
I flew above the crowd in a cross-legged position,
down corridors embroidered with my
dazzled neural matter. And all those arms,
adrift like wheatstalks in a storm, reached up
to touch the flank of something bright, and warm.

Talking 'bout my generation,
that got our instructions for living
from the lyrics of rock and roll
then blasted off into the future
with our eardrums full of scar tissue
and a ridiculous belief in good vibrations.

God of micrograms and decibels,
shirtless deity of drum solos and dance,
you fooled us good
over and over,

and we found out, again and again,
you couldn't hold a bolt of lightning
very long
you couldn't spend a lifetime
on the spire of a moment's exultation.
But the lit-up sign that says **Now Playing**
on the back wall of the brain
still leads me down
to that small illuminated stage,

and I swear that he's still standing there,
the skinny figure in a tank top and old jeans—
a glittering guitar raised in his right hand
like a beacon on a psychedelic tower—
I can hear the thunder and the reverb

while the band plays on,
I can taste the drugs and candy-colored light—

and the adolescent hunger for *more life more life more life*

still flashing, still calling out

like a warning, and a summons.

TONY HOAGLAND

BETWEEN TAKES

I was standing in for myself, my own stunt double,
in a scene where I was meant to do a double

or maybe even a triple back somersault
off the bed. In one hand she held a glass of Meursault.

in the other something akin to a Consulate.
When she spoke, she spoke through the consolette

in a dinner booth where Meatloaf and The Platters
still larded it over those meat-loaf platters

with all the trimmings. This was a moment,
it seemed, of such moment

that she felt obliged to set down both cigarette and glass
and peer as through the limo's tainted glass

for a glimpse of the mountain stream that, bolder and bolder,
did its little bit of laundry among the boulders.

PAUL MULDOON

WATCHING YOUNG COUPLES
WITH AN OLD GIRLFRIEND
ON SUNDAY MORNING

How mild these young men seem to me now
with their baggy shorts and clouds of musk,
as if younger brothers of the women they escort
in tight black leather, bangs and tattoos,
cute little toughies, so Louise Brooks annealed

in MTV, headed off for huevos rancheros
and the Sunday *Times* at some chic, crowded dive.
I don't recall it at all this way, do you?
How sweetly complected and confident they look,
their faces unclouded by the rages

and abandoned, tearful couplings of the night before,
the drunkenness, beast savor and remorse.
Or do I recoil from their youthfulness and health?
Oh, not recoil, just fail to see ourselves.
And yet, this tenderness between us that remains

was mortared first with a darkness that got loose, a frenzy,
we still, we still refuse to name.

AUGUST KLEINZAHLER

MONTAGE: MTV

The way the lotus pushes up
Through the watery mulch and shit,
The day outruns each character
From *The Book of the Dead.*

The heart's weighted for the Eater.
In the corner of the left eye
Three coeds sun on the grass.
Their eyes go back to Pilgrim's Point,

& two steps later, I'm the bellhop
who serves whiskey in *Black Boy.*
But somewhere behind this summer day
Lee Morgan's trumpet pulls me

Beyond their fears & needs.
I hear Frantz Fanon's voice
Just before I unlock my front door
& slip into the arms of Sakhmet.

YUSEF KOMUNYAKAA

THE VICTIM

Oh dead punk lady with the knack
Of looking fierce in pins and black,
The suburbs wouldn't want you back.

You wished upon a shooting star
And trusted in your wish as far
As he was famous and bizarre.

The band broke up, its gesture made.
And though the music stopped, you stayed.
Now it was the sharp things he played:

Needles and you, not with the band,
Till something greater than you planned
Opened erect within his hand.

You smiled. He pushed it through your shirt
Deep in your belly, where it hurt.
You turned, and ate the carpet's dirt.

And then not understanding why

He watched out with a heavy eye
The several hours you took to die.

The news was full of his fresh fame.
He OD'd ending up the same.
Poor girl, poor girl, what was your name?

THOM GUNN

PUNK ROCK YOU'RE MY BIG CRYBABY

I'll tell my deaf mother on you! Fall on the floor
and eat your grandmother's diapers! Drums,
Whatta lotta Noise you want a Revolution?
Wanna Apocalypse? Blow up in Dynamite Sound?
I can't get excited, Louder! Viciouser!
Fuck me in the ass! Suck me! Come in my ears!
I want those pink Abdominal bellybuttons!
Promise you'll murder me in the gutter with Orgasms!
I'll buy a ticket to your nightclub, I wanna get busted!
50 years old I wanna Go! With whips & chains & leather!
Spank me! Kiss me in the eye! Suck me all over
From Mabuhay Gardens to CBGB's coast to coast
Skull to toe Gimme yr electric guitar naked,
Punk President, eat up the FBI w/ yr big mouth.

MABUHAY GARDENS, MAY 1977

ALLEN GINSBERG

ROCK MUSIC

Sex is a Nazi. The students all knew
this at your school. To it, everyone's subhuman
for parts of their lives. Some are all their lives.
You'll be one of those if these things worry you.

The beautiful Nazis, why are they so cruel?
Why, to castrate the aberrant, the original, the wounded
who might change our species and make obsolete
the true race. Which is those who never leave school.

For the truth, we are silent. For the flattering dream,
in massed farting reassurance, we spasm and scream,
but what is a Nazi but sex pitched for crowds?

It's the Calvin SS: you are what you've got
and you'll wrinkle and fawn and work after you're shot
though tears pour in secret from the hot indoor clouds.

LES MURRAY

"WHAT'S SO FUNNY 'BOUT PEACE, LOVE AND UNDERSTANDING"

At the party she said
"You only want what you can't have,"
as you smashed into a locked door.
Give up. The telephone's exploding
With all the wrong numbers, and,
Yes, the blank wall's fascinating,
So who needs sleep?

Here's someone breathing
Appropriate exhortations in your ear,
Here's someone else
With a twelve-in-one-knife,
Here's the boy in the deli
Calling you "sir"
As he wraps the roast beef.

I remember adolescence.
It went by in a blur of hallucinogens,
Peace signs, and speechlessness: days,
Hot beach, then the beach at night:

That perfect sleep sound,
And the stars,
Like pushpins in really lovely material.

ROBERT LONG

MANHATTAN DIPTYCH

I.   BLACK LIGHT

It wasn't enough he was in love
With Ultra Violet after seeing her once
In the Warhol spread in *Ramparts*
No he actually if accidentally ran into her
In the street outside *Max's Kansas City*
In the twisted early hours just before dawn & heaven
Which he said later never looked closer as

She dragged him along with her friends
This sick new puppy from the sticks
With nothing to recommend him but his job
At Bergdorf's & his good looks
& sensational tan which he soon discovered
Looked in the black light of the night's party
As if he'd been painted with chocolate wax

II.   GOLDEN SHOWERS

It was one of those old claw-footed tubs
That sit in the middle of the kitchen

In ancient Manhattan apartments usually
Covered by a board to help disguise
Such cramped utility & all the lights
In the place were off so she was lit
Only by the pulsing neon of the various
Signs hung along the side of her building
& the one opposite

                          each flashing name signifying
Some virtue on the street below & she sat naked
Then reclining in the tub as I stood
Inside it & above her & as she closed her eyes
In something like rapture she teased again
"Ok asshole, now piss on me. . . ."

DAVID ST. JOHN

LUCIFER IN STARLIGHT

TIRED OF HIS DARK DOMINION . . .

—GEORGE MEREDITH

It was something I'd overheard
One evening at a party; a man I liked enormously
        Saying to a mutual friend, a woman
Wearing a vest embroidered with scarlet and violet tulips
      That belled below each breast, "Well, I've always
Preferred Athens; Greece seems to me a country
        Of the day—Rome, I'm afraid, strikes me
As being a city of the night . . ."
      Of course, I knew instantly just what he meant—
        Not simply because I love
Standing on the terrace of my apartment on a clear evening
      As the constellations pulse low in the Roman sky,
The whole mind of night that I know so well
        Shimmering in its elaborate webs of infinite,
Almost divine irony. No, and it wasn't only that Rome
      Was *my* city of the night, that it was here I'd chosen
        To live when I grew tired of my ancient life
As the Underground Man. And it wasn't that Rome's darkness

Was of the kind that consoles so many

Vacancies of the soul; my Rome, with its endless history

Of falls . . . No, it was that this dark was the deep sensual dark

Of the dreamer; this dark was like the violet fur

Spread to reveal the illuminated nipples of

The She-Wolf—all the sequins above in sequence,

The white buds lost in those fields of ever-deepening gentians,

A dark like the polished back of a mirror,

The pool of the night scalloped and hanging

Above me, the inverted reflection of a last,

Odd narcissus . . .

One night my friend Nico came by

Close to three A.M.—As we drank a little wine, I could see

The black of her pupils blown wide,

The spread ripples of the opiate night . . . And Nico

Pulled herself close to me, her mouth almost

Touching my mouth, as she sighed, "Look . . . ,"

And deep within the pupil of her left eye,

Almost like the mirage of a ship's distant, hanging

Lantern rocking with the waves,

I could see, at the most remote end of the receding,

Circular hallway of her eye, there, at its doorway,

At the small aperture of the black telescope of the pupil,
                    A tiny, dangling crucifix—
Silver, lit by the ragged shards of starlight, reflecting
          In her as quietly as pain, as simply as pain . . .
Some years later, I saw Nico on stage in New York, singing
          Inside loosed sheets of shattered light, a fluid
Kaleidoscope washing over her—the way any naked,
                    Emerging Venus steps up along the scalloped lip
Of her shell, innocent and raw as fate, slowly
Obscured by a florescence that reveals her simple, deadly
                    Love of sexual sincerity . . .
          I didn't bother to say hello. I decided to remember
The way in Rome, out driving at night, she'd laugh as she let
          Her head fall back against the cracked, red leather
                    Of my old Lancia's seats, the soft black wind
Fanning her pale, chalky hair out along its currents,
          Ivory waves of starlight breaking above us in the leaves;
The sad, lucent malevolence of the heavens, falling . . .
                    Both of us racing silently as light. Nowhere,
Then forever . . .
                    Into the mind of the Roman night.

DAVID ST. JOHN

C TRAIN HOME: LOU REED AFTER THE WAKE
OF DELMORE SCHWARTZ, JULY 1966

Strangeness woke in the motionless air. Turtleneck
Black, shades black, my best black jeans.
                                              Their heads

All turned to eye me at the open casket
Where Delmore lay propped, waxen and "beflowered,"

Grist now for some Ouija board. The 'ludes
I'd done were coming on. The room went numb:

Narcoleptic voice of Dwight McDonald
Laboring through the eulogy.
                                    On the C train home,

Three greasers razz a colored maid. The little shits'
Switchblades singe the air—they just want to torment her.

No cuts, just thrills. They hop off at 35th.
We torture others or ourselves. *Delmore*—

You taught that lesson best, and lived your sullen art
To death.
                Teacher! Asshole! Here's where I get out.

DAVID WOJAHN

7-MINUTE SONG

Before he left but after he let
me undo the snaps he looked
at me through a porthole said
I forgive you put this light in
your mouth and maybe I'd have
taken that from Lou Reed at 21
down by the piers the Hudson
red as the boat against which
he'd pin me and pull
the river over my head.

MARK BIBBINS

THE PROPHET'S SONG

Chunky on the shag rug, I'm looking for my anthem, I'm looking for my headphones, I'm looking for the bare spot on the rug to wallow, side-stepped on the chair-stopped door. I blast my ears out.

I'm looking at pictures of you, my Catholic prince, my mother-father proxy, I'm in London—the koi pond, the flamingo, the statues, the hymnal, the Aretha Franklin song at the funeral. Alone on a pew, I watch the water.

I'm watching the bare spot on the rug, filled with pictures on the floor, I'm ignoring the knocks on the door. I'm ignoring the knocks on the door. Stepped and stripped on the chair-stopped door. I'm listening, listening.

DANIEL NESTER

THE PROPHECY

The minister's enunciations cut like knives.
He laid his great hand, pale and freckled,
on my shoulder, and made his prophecy.
I stood in my tie and white choir robe
and blushed. The truth was not so much
that I didn't love rock and roll,
but that I loved even more my father's jazz,
songs full of smoke and whiskey, ache and want.
Someday, he said, I would be a preacher,
and my parents behind me grinned, nervous
with the lie we'd not quite told.

The truth is, I didn't give a damn
what we sang, as long as we were singing.
We wondered why the rest of it
couldn't be abandoned: the crazed
responsive readings printed in the programs,
the rot of sermons and their barely veiled threats,
that hell we knew early on
we'd likely never avoid. Soprano boys,
we kept our voices one last year

above the cracks, three of us

in the sacristy drinking communion wine

with Debra, giggling and large-breasted

and lonely. Button by button, hook

by hook, she slowly slipped the robe

from her shoulders, opened her blouse

and lifted the loosened bra from her breasts.

No papery wafer tasted so rich

with salvation, no catechism felt so true.

And Sundays thereafter we sang

with the conviction of saints and met each week

in the sacristy for the confirmation of our flesh.

Still, the truth is a blade and cuts.

We feared the minister, though he owned a dozen suits.

Debra kissed us and laughed. In that room

we couldn't have sung for anything,

not for heaven, not for the hell of fear or betrayal,

not for one last touch the day Debra

declined to bare herself to us,

but only drank, sip and sip, all of us grown

quiet in the glowering, half-holy light.

By Easter our voices were ragged with baritone,

we'd given ourselves over to dancing and drums,
the searing violence of electric guitars,
behind which we wailed and sang.

ROBERT WRIGLEY

BOHEMIAN RHAPSODY

As if in my own benediction ceremony, I would lay out all of the Queen albums, flush next to each other, in order of release, on my bedroom floor. The 45s from each album would lay on top of them, in the lower right-hand corner, also in order of release, from bottom to top.

I would then stand in front of this, drinking a wine cooler, as if I were Noah in the *Ten Commandments* movie, congratulating myself, clasping my arms behind my back, as if this was my ark, my own creation; that I had, as if through my sheer accumulation and arrangement of these objects, some part in creating them.

Actually, back then, I am sure that I thought I had created them, at least in the form of the configuration I was looking at, and the Bartles & Jaymes tasted sweet going down my throat, and with my room clean and vacuumed, I would lie on my bed, jerking off.

DANIEL NESTER

VINCE NEIL MEETS JOSH IN A CHINESE RESTAURANT IN MALIBU (AFTER EZRA POUND)

Back when my voicebox
was a cabinet-full of golden vibrators, and my hair
fell white across the middle of my back
like a child's wedding dress,
I made love to at least a dozen girls
dressed up to look like me: the hotel bed a sky
filled with the spastic flock
of our South-Flying mic scarves,
the back of my head and the front
appearing simultaneously
in hotel mirrors, and the twin crusts of our make-up
sliding off into dangerous satin seas
like bits of California coast. I heard my own lyrics
coming out of the greasy tent
of their cheapo wigs, my lyrics driven back
towards me, poled into me, demanding of me
the willing completion of vague circus acts
I'd scribbled down, once, on the back of a golf card
or a piece of toilet paper. Sometimes I myself
wonder what I was thinking then, but those words
went on to live forever, didn't they, radioed out

into the giant Midwestern backseat
and blasted into kneecaps and tailbones
by that endless tongue of berber carpeting
blanketing the American suburbs, boys and girls
strung like paper lanterns from here to Syracuse
along my microphone cord. Who rocks you now
rocks you always, I told them all,
and all of them somehow wearing
a homemade version of the same leather pants
I'd chosen to wear on stage that night;
all of them hoping to enter me—to enter anyone—
the way they thought I entered them,
and the way I entered them was wishing
I was somewhere else, or wishing I was
the someone else who'd come along
to enter me, which was the same thing.
I am no fag, my new friend.
Love in battle conditions requires a broad
taxonomy, queerness has its ever-more-visible degrees.

Josh, I know you know what I'm talking about,
you have the build of a stevedore. Which reminds me—more shrimp
fried rice?—as a child in Nanjing,
I sculled the junks for my bread and I slept

in a hovel along the Chiang Jiang River.
In a cage there, I bred mice who built their nests
from the frayed rope I'd taken from the decks, and one Spring,
when the babies did not emerge, I lifted
up the rock that hid them, and I found
they'd grown together, fused with each other
and the tendrils of the nest. I held them up, eleven blind tomatoes
wriggling on a blackened vine. My friends and I
performed many surgeries. And now you come to me
in this Chinese restaurant in Malibu,
asking if you can help me. Please tell *Circus Magazine* I love them
forever, and please pass Pamela this message:
If you get back to Malibu by springtime, drop by the boathouse,
and I'll rock your ass as far as Cho-Fu-Sa.

JOSH BELL

VARIATION ON A THEME BY WHITESNAKE

The career taking off was a thing of beauty.
I told you it almost had me convinced.
Though in the public mind it's credible
for a rock star to segue into a movie star
than the other way around
they don't make the rules.
Sure enough the label would screw us out of everything,

but for now the guitar solo was over.
I said, "Baby I hope this repeats and fades out
like the song that's on, with the song that's on."
That must've meant something special because you wrote it down and
later sang it back to me
over a sea of lighters against the concrete stadium walls.
Or later wrote it and sang it like you made it up.

DAN HOY

THE SECRET HISTORY OF ROCK & ROLL

—FOR STEPHEN DUNN

Elvis Presley, Bo Diddley, Bill Haley & the Comets
were lies created on recording tape by the same Group
who made The Bomb, with the same motive:
rule the world. The Little Richard tunes

that made my five-year-old legs bounce and twitch,
and sent me skidding around the dinner table
screaming "Ooh my soul!" and "Woo!" were drugs
poured in my ears to make me despise Sunday School.

Jerry Lee Lewis's marriage to his 13-year-old cousin,
and Chuck Berry's violating the "Man Act"
were lies to make Rock seem more true. Buddy Holly,
Richie Valens, the Big Bopper died when their three

robots blew up in a thunderstorm. In 1962,
I bought a ten-dollar guitar, and squandered
homework time strumming "Little Deuce Coupe."
Dreaming of surfer girls, I joined a "Mersey"

band in '65, faked a British accent, and got swats
at school for past-the-collar hair. My parents' truth
was no match for the Beatles & Rolling Stones hoax,
the Kinks & Yardbirds & Zombies sham.

Vietnam was a staged backdrop for their songs.
Only the fact that every kid my age was equally
impaired let me squeeze into college, where my band,
Lethe, made me forget English, Physics, History,

As Cream, Led Zeppelin, Spirit, Hendrix, Sergeant
Pepper marched me toward burned draft cards
in a "purple haze." When, after Woodstock,
Dad threatened to hold me down and cut my hair,

I said "Try it," and left to play guitar full-time.
The Group's World War II masterminds
were dying out, but their successors created
Johnny Rotten, David Bowie, Kiss, and Queen,

While I fought to get my "sound" onto vinyl,
never dreaming that the record companies
who sent back encouraging Nos,
were mail drops just like those to Santa Claus.

Disco gave me a good long look at the The Lie.
I quit my band, married, and got a job
teaching Psychology. The Yngwe Malmsteen
android made me pick my "ax" back up,

and relearn a few licks. Emotion roused
by ZZ Top's "Can't Stop Rocking" caused
the fight that unmarried me in '92,
and made me swear I'd quit the U and hit the road

But sense prevailed. Now, though my feet still tap,
I see Rap, Hip Hop, Grunge, and Techno-Rock
for what they are. The decay preachers railed
against when "Elvis" shook goes on.

I barely know my country anymore.
The Group has won. But I've escaped. One kid
who lived for Rock has seen the light.
My brain was not my own. I renounce that boy.

CHARLES HARPER WEBB

MOSTLY MICK JAGGER

1

Thank god he stuck his tongue out.
When I was twelve I was in danger
of taking my body seriously.
I thought the ache in my nipple was priceless.
I thought I should stay very still
and compare it to a button,
a china saucer,
a flash in a car side-mirror,
so I could name the ache either big or little,
then keep it forever. He blew no one a kiss,
then turned into a maw.

After I saw him, when a wish moved in my pants,
I nurtured it. I stalked around my room
kicking my feet up just like him, making
a big deal of my lips. I was my own big boy.
I wouldn't admit it then,
but he definitely cocks his hip
as if he is his own little girl.

2

People ask me—I make up interviews
while I brush my teeth—"So, what do you remember best
about your childhood?" I say
mostly the drive toward Chicago.
Feeling as if I'm being slowly pressed against the skyline.
Hoping to break a window.
Mostly quick handfuls of boys' skin.
Summer twilights that took forever to get rid of.
Mostly Mick Jagger.

3

How do I explain my hungry stare?
My Friday night spent changing clothes?
My love for travel? I rewind the way he says "now"
With so much roof of the mouth.
I rewind until I get a clear image of myself:
I'm telling the joke he taught me
about my body. My mouth is stretched open
so I don't laugh. My hands are pretending
to have just discovered my own face.
My name is written out in metal studs
across my little pink jumper.

I've got a mirror and a good idea
of the way I want my face to look.
When I glance sideways my smile should twitch
as if a funny picture of me is taped up
inside the corner of my eye.
A picture where my hair is combed over each shoulder,
my breasts are well-supported, and my teeth barely show.
A picture where I'm trying hard to say "beautiful."

He always says "This is my skinny rib cage,
my one, two chest hairs."
That's all he ever says.
Think of a bird with no feathers
or think of a hundred lips bruising every inch of his skin.
There are no pictures of him hoping
he said the right thing.

CATIE ROSEMURGY

NECROMANCY: THE LAST DAYS OF BRIAN JONES, 1968

Hair fanning out, he'll float upside down,
Like the end, and beginning, of *Sunset Boulevard*.
Kicked out of the band, he's come home
To his manor in St. John's Wood—acid,

Hard drugs, delivered by minions to poolside,
Where for months on the nod he strums his National Steel,
Sprawled on a Day-Glo deck chair, lavender strobes
Festooning the water. He'll drown on his last meal,

Then fall to the chlorined deep end. But today he's dressed
As a wizard, star-checked robe and pointed cap,
Cover props from *His Satanic Majesty's Request*.
A syringe and phone are on his lap

But who does the necromancer call? Dial tone.
Hair fanning out, he'll float upside down.

DAVID WOJAHN

GIMME SHELTER

The thread or the theme
That holds this tune
Together is the same
One that rips it open—

The initial guitar
Continues splitting
The whole thing apart–
It is the lightning

Which Jagger complains
Of and which he seeks
Shelter from the rains
Of when it breaks—

We ourselves will shut
Our deepest sills against
His common cries but
There is no defense

To keep out that other
One behind him twinned

His starker brother
Whose keening strings skein

Hymns from one more
Murderous composer
Whose cause is war
Who tears down our door—

Shelter/the home
Is made of language—
But music sunders the poem—
Its rift is like a tongue

Trying to compile all
Words into one word—
One Babel whose walls
Fall beneath its standard—

What the fuck did that flag
Say—the opposite
Of peace/of the page
Is what I must write.

BILL KNOTT

THE PENALTY FOR BIGAMY IS TWO WIVES

I don't understand how Janis Joplin did it, how she made her voice
break out like that in hives of feeling. I have a friend who writes poems
who says he really wants to be a rock star—the high-heeled boots, the
hand-held mike, the glare of underpants in the front row, the whole
package. He says he likes the way music throws you back into your
body, like organic food or heroin. But when he sings it is sleek and
abstract except for the pain, like the silhouette of a dog baying at the
moon, almost liver-shaped, a bell hung from a rope of its own pure
yearning. Naturally his life is exciting, but sometimes I think he can't tell
the difference between salvation and death. When I listen to my Janis
Joplin records I think of him. Once I got drunk & sloppy and told him I
feared artists always had more fun and more death, too, and how I had
these strong feelings but nothing to do with them and he said *Don't
worry I'd trade my onion collection for a good cry, wouldn't you?* I didn't
really understand but poetry is how you feel so I lie back and listen to
Janis's dead voice run up and down my body like a fire that has learned
to live on itself and I think *Here it comes, Grief's beautiful blow job.*
I think about the painter who was said to paint with his penis and I
imagine one of his portraits letting down a local rain of hair around
his penis now too stiff to paint with, as if her diligent silence meant to
say *You loved me enough to make me, when will I see you next?* Janis,

I don't care what anybody thinks or writes, I don't care if my friend who writes poems is a beautiful fake, like a planetarium ceiling, I want to hold my life in my arms as easily as my body will forever hold the silence for which the mouth slowly opens.

WILLIAM MATTHEWS

YOU CAN'T RHUMBOOGIE IN A BALL AND CHAIN

(FOR JANIS JOPLIN)

You called the blues' loose black belly lover
and in Port Arthur they called you pig-face.
The way you chugged booze straight, without a glass,
your brass-assed language, slingbacks with jeweled heel,
proclaimed you no kin to their muzzled blood.
No chiclet-toothed Baptist boyfriend for you.

Strung-out, street hustling showed men wouldn't buy you.
Once you clung to the legs of a lover,
let him drag you till your knees turned to blood,
mouth hardened to a thin scar on your face,
cracked under songs, screams, never left to heal.
Little Girl Blue, soul pressed against the glass.

That voice rasping like you'd guzzled fiber-glass,
stronger than the four armed men behind you.
But pale horse lured you, docile, to heel:
warm snow flanks pillowed you like a lover.
Men feared the black holes in your body and face,
knew what they put in would return as blood.

Craving fast food, cars, garish as fresh blood,

diners with flies and doughnuts under glass,
Formica bars and a surfer's gold face,
in nameless motels, after sign-off, you
let TV's blank bright stare play lover,
lay still, convinced its cobalt rays could heal.

Your songs that sound ground under some stud's heel,
swallowed and coughed up in a voice like blood:
translation unavailable, lover!
No prince could shoe you in unyielding glass,
stories of exploding pumpkins bored you
who flaunted tattooed breast and hungry face.

That night needing a sweet-legged sugar's face,
a hot, sky-eyed Southern comfort to heal
the hurt of senior proms for all but you,
plain Janis Lyn, self-hatred laced your blood.
You knew they worshipped drained works, emptied glass,
legend's last gangbang the wildest lover.

Like clerks we face your image in the glass,
suggest lovers, as accessories, heels.
"It's your shade, this blood dress," we say. "It's you."

ALICE FULTON

PEARL

SHE WAS A HEADLONG ASSAULT, A HYSTERICAL DISCHARGE,

AN ACT OF TOTAL EXTERMINATION.

—MYRA FRIEDMAN, *BURIED ALIVE:*

THE BIOGRAPHY OF JANIS JOPLIN

She was nothing much, this plain-faced girl from Texas,
this moonfaced child who opened her mouth
to the gravel pit churning in her belly, acne-faced
daughter of Leadbelly, Bessie, Otis, and the booze-
filled moon, child of the honky-tonk bar-talk crowd
who cackled like a bird of prey, velvet cape blown
open in the Monterey wind, ringed fingers fisted
at her throat, howling the slagheap up and out
into the sawdusted air. Barefaced, mouth warped
and wailing like giving birth, like being eaten alive
from the inside, or crooning like the first child
abandoned by God, trying to woo him back,
down on her knees and pleading for a second chance.
When she sang she danced a stand-in-place dance,
one foot stamping at that fire, that bed of coals;
one leg locked at the knee and quivering, the other

pumping its oil-rig rhythm, her bony hip jigging
so the beaded belt slapped her thigh.
Didn't she give it to us? So loud so hard so furious,
hurling heat-seeking balls of lightning
down the long human aisles, her voice crashing
into us—sonic booms to the heart—this little white girl
who showed us what it was like to die
for love, to jump right up and die for it night after
drumbeaten night, going down shrieking—hair
feathered, frayed, eyes glazed, addicted to the song—
a one-woman let me show you how it's done, how it is,
where it goes when you can't hold it in anymore.
Child of everything gone wrong, gone bad, gone down,
gone. Girl with the girlish breasts and woman hips,
thick-necked, sweat misting her upper lip, hooded eyes
raining a wild blue light, hands reaching out
to the ocean we made, all that anguish and longing
swelling and rising at her feet. Didn't she burn
herself up for us, shaking us alive? That child,
that girl, that rawboned woman, stranded
in a storm on a blackened stage like a house
on fire.

DORIANNE LAUX

BERKELEY 1971

I woke this morning, remembering
a small white dog from long ago.

It was waiting in its cage at the pet store
every day when I'd go in. It stayed

locked up, while children pulled puppies
out onto linoleum, wrestled with them

on the cold and musty floor. I debated
and debated but never brought it home.

Then this evening at a party, they played
old Linda Ronstadt tunes. "I've done everything I know

to try and make you mine," one song moaned
and moaned again, 'til I broke into tears. A friend,

said it was because Ronstadt sang it
in a minor key. But I was back in Berkeley yet again.

There, in the crash pad a floor below
my room, a girl, 15, a runaway, wailed

and cried most every night. Hour after hour,
her record player blared, "And I think it's gonna hurt me

for a long, long time." It groaned on well past midnight
until, near dawn, I marched downstairs.

When I found her shaking, naked, by the open window,
I backed away. Then later, feeling foolish,

I came back with hot chocolate and a blanket,
tried to tuck her into flimsy sheets. She was just bones,

not much more, on a soiled mattress on the floor.
In the small white face, the eyes focused nowhere.

KAREN GLENN

BLUE LONELY DREAMS

Hi Roy. Hope all is well;
just wanted to drop a line
to let you know we miss you.
Down here, sand is falling,
and it's slack and spare,
pleading in a whisper
that sweeps the leaves
into the drainage gutter,
and shrieks in a slow winded high note
that is not falsetto, but a voice
truly able to hit this note.

How goes the opera, upstairs?
Is it as good as touring the country
and singing for strangers
who care for you and your music?
Now the ghostly words
in the ghostly librettos
are ghosts themselves,
disguised as snowflakes
and floating in the air like a raft on the bayou,
distilled before reaching the ground.

We had tickets for the original
February date at the Beacon.
I had read an article about your induction
into The Rock and Roll Hall of Fame,
and was pleased to learn
that we were both born on April 23rd.

On the day of the concert,
the doctor said they would have to operate
on my mother's lung cancer.
She stayed with us that night,
insisting that we go to see you play.
I didn't know how I was going to get through it,
but I knew it would be best for everyone if we went.
When we reached the theatre, the marquee read:
TONIGHT'S SHOW CANCELLED. I couldn't believe it:
the immediate feeling was one of voodoo,
or magic, or a shared faith.
It was like being forgiven
for a mistake you were allowed to make,
but hadn't made. The ushers at the door
told us that your throat was sore;
the voice you had loved from the first time

you heard it; the passion you had balanced
with a preacher man's stance.

On March 10th, two days
before the rescheduled concert,
my mother was given a clean bill of health.
Radiation treatments and chemotherapy
would not be needed.
The show you did on Saturday night
was another answered prayer,
and served as a reminder
why other prayers are better left unanswered.
By then, we considered you a good friend.
Who could grasp what depths
your voice was coming from?
It was as familiar and otherly
as a lone tree on a huge, rolling plain.
The walls of The Beacon were swaying,
and the red and white notes were birds
lifted into the cerulean air.

And here you are today,
on the cover of the new issue of *Rolling Stone:*

black glasses, black shirt and black hair.
Nice of you to drop by on this,
our last day at 51 West 68th Street.
I was just writing you a letter,
and was going to close by complaining
about how traumatic moving is.
By this time tomorrow,
we'll be living downtown.
I just finished reading your last interview.
Life's a bitch, but it's funny, ain't it?
I mean, with The Traveling Wilburys' collaboration,
and a new album of your own
set for February release,
along with a planned tour to support it,
and you up and die.

I guess no matter how many times it comes,
success is always a little bit too early or too late.
But in your wisdom, and in the short, full range
of your emotional wilderness,
you looked at it differently:
one must continue to do what one must do,
though meaning and purpose might seem to vanish

20,000 Leagues Under the Sea.
Time barks, the rooster crows,
and both beliefs resurface
with nothing having changed
and everything further revealed.

I've got a lot to learn
about taking things in stride,
but as you said, I'm not alone anymore,
only terribly lonely.
Once again, thanks for stopping by.
If there's anything we can do for you,
just holler. If I get the chance,
and wind up upstairs some day,
I look forward to hearing you sing
"Blue Lonely Dreams," that quintessential song
you spoke about writing in the interview.

Take care, Roy, be well. I hope the girl
who's coming to pack the cartons
is dark, mysterious and beautiful.
After all, death is out there somewhere,
squaring its shoulders, dancing the bolero

and growling like a tiger
lying among the reeds;
but too much has happened already,
and though not enough is never more,
an image can ease the pain.
I feel more for the stray kitten at the doorstep
than I fear death. The pitch of the wind ripping
through the reeds is a crescendo rising
interminably above the previous crescendo.
At the window, the sunshine is making the leaves shine.
The doorbell breaks my concentration,
and I open the door and all my hopes are realized,
On a day when it feels good to be alive
in an apartment that will be empty tomorrow,
and already in thought, was once ours,
the girl says she's not allergic to dust
as I sneeze and rejoice in the bloodstained minutes
that fall upon the white ocean,
that sink below the blue sea.

MARC COHEN

COMEBACKS

The Eagles pack houses each time they return—but smaller
houses, the ones who pack them, grayer every year.
Once a month, Zeppelin's Jimmy Page kicks "junk,"

and picks up a new singer, though none achieves
the stratospheric shrieks of Robert Plant in '69.
His comebacks scare me: gullied face and raven-grak . . .

Roy Orbison's throat was more relaxed, his voice sweeter
than in his prime, the day a heart attack yanked him
off the comeback trail for good. The Rolling Stones refuse

to roll away. But the saddest comebacks have nowhere
to go—like drunks in bars who won't stop yakking—
like exes who must be dragged, weeping and thrashing,

off love's stage. The boozy guitar man slumped
next to me in Denny's can't believe he laid down his last
number one, shoved out the door by a boy who man-

handles his record company like Daddy's Testarosa. So

easy to say, "Why can't the whiner just stride proudly
into that dark night?" Easy to hoot, when no crowds howled

"Encore!" for you. Easy to love the nose-dives of the great,
driven lower by their heights than we who fight to keep
alive the joys of Maui in '95, the thrill of Joan in '59,

that belly-laugh with Frank, mired in Germany, 1944.
Isn't every song, novel, movie, painting, poem a plea?
Come back, Johnny. Come back, blue Datsun with candy-

striped canopy. Thirty-inch waist, come back. Bring more
of your Hershey kisses, Carla, to Oaks Drive-In, *Horror
of Dracula* receding as, in the back seat of Dad's gray Ford,

we settled down to feed. Wake me to oatmeal and toast
with cherry jam, my clothes laid out, my Tarzan lunchbox
packed—oh Mommy, Daddy, please. Come back.

CHARLES HARPER WEBB

BIRTHDAY

I make my way down the back stairs
in the dark. I know
it sounds crude to admit it,
but I like to piss in the back yard.

You can be alone for a minute
and look up at the stars,
and when you return
everyone is there.

You get drunker, and listen to records.
Everyone agrees.
The dead singers have the best voices.
At four o'clock in the morning

the dead singers have the best voices.
And I can hear them now,
as I climb the stairs
in the dark I know.

FRANZ WRIGHT

POET BIOGRAPHIES

PATIENCE AGBABI is a UK-based poet. Since 1990 she has performed her work on TV and radio. Her most recent collection is *Transformatrix* and she is currently working on her third collection, *Bloodshot Monochrome.*

ROBIN BEHN is the author of *Paper Bird* and coeditor of *The Practice of Poetry: Writing Exercises from Poets Who Teach.* Behn teaches in the creative writing program at the University of Alabama in Tuscaloosa.

JOSH BELL'S first book is *No Planets Strike,* published by Zoo Press. He is a Ph.D. candidate in English at the University of Cincinnati, where he is University Distinguished Graduate Fellow.

MARK BIBBINS teaches writing workshops at the New School, where he also cofounded *LIT magazine.* His work has appeared in *Poetry,* the *Paris Review,* and the *Yale Review. sky lounge* is his first collection of poetry.

KURT BROWN has published three collections of poetry and his fourth, *Future Ship,* was published by Story Line Press in 2006. He has also edited several anthologies, including *Conversation Pieces: Poems That Talk to Other Poems* from Alfred A. Knopf, in the Everyman's Library Pocket Poets, in 2007.

MARC COHEN was born in Brooklyn and raised on Long Island. He is the author of *On Maplewood Time* and his work has appeared in three editions of *The Best American Poetry.* He served as an editor for the Intuflo Chapbook Series and was awarded grants from the Fund for Poetry in 1990 and 1992.

BILLY COLLINS is the author of numerous books of poetry, including *Picnic, Lightning* and *The Art of Drowning.* Collins's poetry has appeared in anthologies, textbooks, and a variety of magazines. He is professor of English at Lehman College, CUNY, and a visiting writer at Sarah Lawrence College. In 2001 he was named the eleventh U.S. Poet Laureate.

MICHAEL DONAGHY was born in New York in 1954 but moved to London in 1985, where he worked as a teacher and musician. His books, *Dances Learned Last Night—Poems 1975-1995* and *Conjure,* were both published by Picador. He died in 2004.

RITA DOVE was born in Ohio in 1952 and attended Miami University in Ohio before receiving her master's degree in 1977 from the Writers' Workshop at the University of Iowa. In 1987, she won the Pulitzer Prize for *Thomas and Beulah,* a collection of poems loosely based on the life of her grandparents. In 1993, she was appointed to a two-year term as Poet Laureate of the United States. She is a professor of English at the University of Virginia in Charlottesville.

NORMAN DUBIE, born in Vermont in 1945, is the author of more than twenty books. He has received numerous prizes, including the Bess Hokin Award of the Modern Poetry Association. Since 1975 he has taught on the faculty of Arizona State University.

CAROL ANN DUFFY was born in Glasgow, Scotland, in 1955. She currently lives in Manchester, where she lectures in poetry for The Writing School at Manchester Metropolitan University. Her collections of poetry have received many awards, including both the Forward Prize and the Whitbread Prize for *Mean Time* (1993).

STEPHEN DUNN is the author of numerous collections of poetry, including *Different Hours,* which won the Pulitzer Prize in 2000. He has most recently published *Loosestrife* and teaches at Richard Stockton College in New Jersey.

JIM ELLEDGE is a poet and chair of the Department of English and Humanities at the Pratt Institute in Brooklyn. His most recent books are *The Chapters of Coming Forth by Day* and the anthologies *Real Things* and *Gay, Lesbian, Bisexual, and Transgendered Myths from the Arapaho to the Zuni: An Anthology.*

B. H. FAIRCHILD is the author of four poetry collections, including *Early Occult Memory Systems of the Lower Midwest*, which won a National

Book Critics Circle Award. Among other honors, he has also received the Kingsley Tufts Award, a Guggenheim Fellowship, and was a finalist for the National Book Award. He lives in Claremont, California.

ROBYN FIALKOW is entering her sophomore year at Boston University, where she is studying classics and philosophy. Voted "Friendliest" in high school, she loves traveling and meeting new people. Robyn wants to thank her family for always supporting and caring for her, and she hopes that everyone can learn from the words of John Lennon and "give peace a chance."

ALICE FULTON has published six books of poetry. The most recent are *Cascade Experiment* (Norton, 2004) and *Felt* (2001). Her work has been included in five editions of *The Best American Poetry*. She is also a recipient of a fellowship from the MacArthur Foundation.

TESS GALLAGHER is a poet, fiction writer, essayist, screenplay writer, and translator. Her poetry collections include *Dear Ghosts, Moon Crossing Bridge*, and *Amplitude: New and Selected Poems*. In 1979 she began living with the short-story writer Raymond Carver, whom she married shortly before his death in 1988.

ALLEN GINSBERG was born in 1926 in Newark, New Jersey, and died in 1997. His most famous poem, *Howl,* was written in 1955. In addition to winning the National Book Award for *The Fall of America: Poems of These*

States, 1965–1971, he was an activist against the Vietnam War and one of the founders of the Beats. In his later years he served as the Grand Old Man of pop counterculture, even appearing in a video for MTV in 1996.

KAREN GLENN'S poems have appeared in *Poetry Northwest, Nimrod,* and many other periodicals. *North American Review* nominated her for a Pushcart Prize. She has been a finalist in the Four Way Books poetry book contest and has read her poetry on NPR's *All Things Considered.*

LAVINIA GREENLAW was born in London in 1962, where she still lives. She worked as a book editor and arts administrator until 1994, and since then has been a freelance writer, reviewer, and radio broadcaster. She teaches in the creative writing MA program at Goldsmiths College, University of London. She has published four poetry collections and several novels.

THOM GUNN was a British poet born in Gravesend, Kent, in 1929. After studying English literature at Trinity College, Cambridge, he published his first collection of verse the following year. In 1954, he emigrated to the United States to teach writing at Stanford University. He died in San Francisco in 2004.

MARK HALLIDAY'S books of poems are *Little Star, Tasker Street, Selfwolf,* and *Jab* (2002). His book on Wallace Stevens, *Stevens and the Interpersonal,* appeared in 1991. He teaches at Ohio University.

EDWARD HIRSCH was born in Chicago in 1950 and attended Grinnell College and the University of Pennsylvania. After teaching at Wayne State University and the University of Houston he became president of the Guggenheim Foundation in 2002. He has published several volumes of poetry and *How to Read a Poem and Fall in Love with Poetry,* which was a best seller in 1999.

TONY HOAGLAND is the author of three volumes of poetry: *Sweet Ruin; Donkey Gospel,* winner of the James Laughlin Award of the Academy of American Poets; and *What Narcissism Means to Me.* He currently teaches in the University of Houston writing program and in the Warren Wilson MFA program.

DAN HOY lives in Brooklyn and is a coeditor of the journal *Soft Targets.*

DAVID HUDDLE'S fiction, essays, and poetry have appeared in *Esquire* and *Harper's* magazine. The recipient of two NEA fellowships, he teaches writing at the University of Vermont and resides in Burlington, Vermont.

LYNDA HULL, who died in 1994, was the author of three volumes of poetry: *Ghost Money, Star Ledger,* and *The Only World.* She was the recipient of fellowships from the National Endowment for the Arts and the Illinois Arts Council and winner of the Carl Sandburg Award.

ALAN JENKINS was born in London in 1955 and works as an editor for the *Times Literary Supplement*. He has published seven volumes of poetry, won numerous awards, and lives in London.

AUGUST KLEINZAHLER was born in Jersey City in 1949. He is the author of ten books of poems, most recently *Green Sees Things in Waves* and *Live from the Hong Kong Nile Club*. His most recent title, *The Strange Hours Travelers Keep,* was published in 2003. He lives in San Francisco.

BILL KNOTT was born in Carson City, Michigan. The author of ten volumes of poetry, including *The Naomi Poems* and *Laugh at the End of the World: Collected Comic Poems, 1969–1999*, he is also a book artist whose handmade, one-of-a-kind volumes are prized by collectors. He teaches at Emerson College.

YUSEF KOMUNYAKAA is the author of eleven books of poems, including *Thieves of Paradise*, a finalist for the National Book Critics Circle Award, and *Neon Vernacular*, winner of the 1994 Pulitzer Prize. He is a professor in the Council of Humanities and Creative Writing program at Princeton University. He lives in New York City.

PHILIP LARKIN was born in Coventry, England, and attended St. John's College, Oxford. With his second volume of poetry, *The Less Deceived* (1955), Larkin became the poet of his generation. In 1964 he confirmed his reputation as a major poet with the publication of *The Whitsun Weddings* and, in 1974, *High Windows*. Larkin was also known as an aficionado and critic of jazz. He died in 1985.

DORIANNE LAUX was born in Augusta, Maine, in 1952. She is the author of three collections of poetry: *Smoke, What We Carry,* and *Awake*. With Kim Addonizio, she is the coauthor of *The Poet's Companion: A Guide to the Pleasures of Writing Poetry* (1997). Laux is an associate professor at the University of Oregon's Program in Creative Writing.

PHILIP LEVINE was born in 1928 in Detroit. For much of his adult life he taught at the University in Fresno, California. He has received many awards for his books of poems, most recently the National Book Award in 1991 for *What Work Is*, and the Pulitzer Prize in 1995 for *The Simple Truth*.

LARRY LEVIS was born in Fresno, California, in 1946, the son of a grape grower. He graduated from Fresno State College in 1968 and went on to earn a Ph.D. from the University of Iowa in 1974. He won numerous awards for his three volumes of poetry, including *The Afterlife* and *The Dollmaker's Ghost*. He died in 1996.

ROBERT LONG'S poems have appeared in many magazines and he has published four collections of poetry. He has taught at several colleges and universities, including La Salle University, where he was writer in residence. He lives in East Hampton, New York.

RODDY LUMSDEN was born in 1966 in St. Andrews, Scotland, and now lives in London, where he works as a freelance editor and reviewer. He has published three collections of poetry, including *Yeah Yeah Yeah* and *Roddy Lumsden Is Dead.*

DEREK MAHON was born in Belfast in 1941, studied at Trinity College, Dublin, and the Sorbonne, and has held journalistic and academic appointments in London and New York. He has received numerous awards, including the Irish Academy of Letters Award and the Scott Moncrieff translation prize.

SARAH MANGUSO lives in Brooklyn and teaches at the Pratt Institute. Her first book, *The Captain Lands in Paradise*, was a Village Voice Favorite Book of the Year. Her second book, *Siste Viator*, was published by Four Way Books.

WILLIAM MATTHEWS published eleven books of poetry and a book of essays in his lifetime. Two posthumous books of his poems—*After All: Last Poems* (1998) and *Search Party: Collected Poems* (2004)—were published after his death in 1997. Matthews's last book of poetry, *Time and Money*, won the National Book Critics Circle Award in 1996.

CAMPBELL MCGRATH is the author of six books of poems, including *Pax Atomica*, his most recent collection. He has received the Kingsley

Tufts Prize and fellowships from the Guggenheim and MacArthur Foundations. He teaches in the creative writing program at Florida International University in Miami.

HEATHER MCHUGH is professor of English at the University of Washington in Seattle and also teaches in the MFA program at Warren Wilson College. She is the author of six books of poetry, including *Eyeshot* (Wesleyan University Press, 2003) and *Hinge & Sign: Poems, 1968-1993* (Wesleyan Poetry Series, 2004).

PAUL MULDOON was born in 1951 in County Armagh, Northern Ireland, and attended Queen's University of Belfast. Since 1987, he has lived in the United States, where he is professor of the humanities at Princeton University. He won the Pulitzer Prize in 2003 for *Moy Sand and Gravel*. His tenth collection, *Horse Latitudes*, appeared in 2006.

LES MURRAY is the author of twelve books of poetry, including *Learning Human: Selected Poems* and *Conscious and Verbal*. His collection *Subhuman Redneck Poems* received the T. S. Eliot Prize, and in 1998 he was awarded the Gold Medal for Poetry presented by Queen Elizabeth II. He lives on a farm on the north coast of New South Wales, Australia.

DANIEL NESTER is a poet, editor, and teacher who lives in Brooklyn, New York. His work has appeared in *The Best American Poetry 2003* and elsewhere. He is the editor of the online literary journal *Unpleasant Event Schedule* and former editor of *La Petite Zine*. *God Save My Queen*, published by Soft Skull Press, is his first collection.

IDRA NOVEY was born in western Pennsylvania and has since lived in Chile, Brazil, and New York. Her selected translations of Brazilian poet Paulo Henriques Britto, winner of a 2004 PEN Translation Fund Award, is forthcoming from BOA Editions. She currently teaches in the Undergraduate Writing Program at Columbia University.

WILLIAM OLSEN'S most recent book of poetry is *Trouble Lights*. Along with Sharon Bryan, he coedited *Planet on the Table: Poets on the Reading Life*. He teaches at Western Michigan University and Vermont College.

VICTORIA REDEL is author of four books, including *Loverboy*, which received several awards and was selected as a 2001 Best Book by the *L.A. Times*. *Swoon*, her most recent collection of poems, was a finalist for the James Laughlin award.

CATIE ROSEMURGY is the author of one book of poems, *My Favorite Apocalypse* (Graywolf, 2001). Her work has also appeared in *Ploughshares*, *Verse, Poetry Northwest,* and other journals. She is coeditor of the *Laurel Review* and teaches English at Northwest Missouri State University.

DAVID ST. JOHN is director of the Ph.D. program in literature and creative writing at the University of Southern California in Los Angeles. He is the author of nine volumes of poetry, most recently *The Face*, as well as a volume of essays, interviews, and reviews. Other collections include *Study for the World's Body, The Red Leaves of Night,* and *Prism*. He has also won numerous awards, including fellowships from the Guggenheim Foundation and the Rome Prize.

CHARLES SIMIC was born in Belgrade, Yugoslavia, in 1938, but moved to New York City when he was sixteen to rejoin his father. He has published over sixty books, including many translations, and won the Pulitzer Prize for *The World Doesn't End: Prose Poems* in 1990. He has won fellowships from the Guggenheim Foundation and MacArthur Foundation and has lived and taught in New Hampshire since 1973.

JAMES TATE was born in Kansas City, Missouri, in 1943. He is the author of twelve collections of poetry. His first volume, *The Lost Pilot,* was selected for the Yale Series of Younger Poets in 1967. In 1992, Tate was awarded the Pulitzer Prize for Poetry for his *Selected Poems*. He has taught at the University of Massachusetts in Amherst since 1971.

DANIEL TOBIN is the author of three books of poems, *Where the World Is Made, Double Life,* and *The Narrows*. He has been widely published in journals and his work has appeared in many anthologies. He is chair of the Department of Writing, Literature, and Publishing at Emerson College.

CHARLES HARPER WEBB's book *Amplified Dog* won the Saltman Prize for Poetry and was published in 2006 by Red Hen Press. Recipient of grants from the Whiting and Guggenheim Foundations, he directs Creative Writing at California State University, Long Beach.

JONATHAN WELLS is the editor of *Third Rail*. His poems have appeared in numerous reviews, including *Hayden's Ferry*, *Nimrod*, and *Poetry International*.

DAVID WOJAHN is the author of six volumes of poetry, including *Mystery Train*, *Late Empire*, and *The Falling Hour*. Wojahn is professor of English and director of the Program in Creative Writing at Indiana University, and a member of the faculty of the MFA in Writing Program of Vermont College.

CHARLES WRIGHT, winner of the Pulitzer Prize, the National Book Critics Circle Award, and the National Book Award, teaches at the University of Virginia in Charlottesville.

FRANZ WRIGHT was born in Vienna in 1953. His most recent works include *The Beforelife* and *Ill Lit: Selected & New Poems*. For his most recent collection, *Walking To Martha's Vineyard* (2004), he was awarded the Pulitzer Prize. He works at the Edinburgh Center for Grieving Children and Teenagers and lives in Waltham, Massachusetts.

ROBERT WRIGLEY'S *Reign of Snakes* won the 2000 Kingsley Tufts Poetry Award. He teaches at the University of Idaho and lives with his wife, the writer Kim Barnes, and their children near Moscow, Idaho.

KEVIN YOUNG has published four collections of poetry and edited three anthologies, among them *Blues Poems* and the forthcoming *Jazz Poems*. *Most Way Home* was selected by Lucille Clifton for the National Poetry Series. Young is currently curator for the Raymond Danowski Poetry Library at Emory University and is completing two more books of poetry.

MATTHEW ZAPRUDER is the author of *American Linden*, published by Tupelo Press, and *The Pajamaist*, published by Copper Canyon in 2006. His poems have appeared or are upcoming in *The Boston Review*, *The New Republic*, and *The New Yorker*, among other periodicals. He lives in New York City and teaches poetry in the MFA Program at the New School.

CREDITS

Larry Levis: "Descrescendo" from *Winter Stars*. Copyright © 1985 by Larry Levis. Reprinted with the permission of the University of Pittsburgh Press.

Robert Long: "Love Potion No. 9" from *Blue* (Canio's Editions). Copyright © 1999 by Robert Lond. "What's So Funny Bout Peace Love and Understanding?" from *What Happens* (Galileo Press). Copyright © 1988 by Robert Long. Both reprinted with the permission of the author.

Roddy Lumsden: "Yeah Yeah Yeah" from *Mischief Night: New & Selected Poems*. Copyright © 2004 by Roddy Lumsden. Reprinted with the permission of Bloodaxe Books, Ltd.

Derek Mahon: "Rock Music" from *Collected Poems*. Copyright © 1999 by Derek Mahon. Reprinted with the permission of the author and The Gallery Press.

Sarah Manguso: "Alas, They Sighed, You Were Not Like Us" from *Siste Viator*. Originally published in *The American Poetry Review* (May/June 2003). Reprinted with the permission of the author.

William Matthews: "An Elegy for Bob Marley" and "The Penalty for Bigamy Is Two Wives" from *Search Party: Collected Poems*. Copyright © 2004 by Sebastian Matthews and Stanley Plumly. Reprinted with the permission of Houghton Mifflin Company.

Campbell McGrath: "Guns N' Roses" from *Pax Atomica*. Copyright © 2004 by Campbell McGrath. Reprinted with the permission of HarperCollins Publishers.

Heather McHugh: "Sleep, After Ray Charles and Hurricane Report" from *Hinge & Sign: Poems, 1968-1993*. Copyright © 1994 by Heather McHugh. Reprinted with the permission of Wesleyan University Press.